Rise of the Revisionists

Rise of the Revisionists

Russia, China, and Iran

Essays by
Gary J. Schmitt • Frederick W. Kagan
Dan Blumenthal • Reuel Marc Gerecht
Walter Russell Mead

Edited by Gary J. Schmitt

THE AEI PRESS

Publisher for the American Enterprise Institute
WASHINGTON, DC

ISBN-13: 978-0-8447-5013-2 (hardback)
ISBN-13: 978-0-8447-5014-9 (paperback)

American Enterprise Institute
1789 Massachusetts Avenue, NW
Washington, DC 20036
www.aei.org

Printed in the United States of America

Contents

Introduction:
The Challenge Ahead

GARY J. SCHMITT

If the vast majority of foreign policy analysts and commentators agree on one thing, it is that "the unipolar moment" has passed. American dominance—be it political, economic, or military—is no longer so overwhelming that history can be said to have ended.[1] To the contrary, the security challenges the US confronts are spread across the globe and are as complex as any the country has faced since its infancy.

While al Qaeda, ISIS, and North Korea present deadly serious problems, America's geopolitical situation is unique in that we are confronted by the rise of revisionist powers in each of the three regions traditionally seen as crucial to our own peace and prosperity and to the larger goal of global stability: Russia in Europe, China in East Asia, and Iran in the Middle East. If the US is to develop effective, sustainable policies that truly serve its national interests, we must first understand the roots and the character of the challenges these three countries pose.

The chapters that follow (Frederick Kagan's "Russia: The Kremlin's Many Revisions," Dan Blumenthal's "China: The Imperial Legacy," and Reuel Marc Gerecht's "Iran: The Shi'ite Imperial Power") attempt to spell out the specific nature of each country's revisionist drive and how, broadly speaking, the US and its allies should respond. The volume concludes with Walter Russell Mead's "Not a Trap but a Minefield: The Thucydidean Challenge to American Foreign Policy," which argues that, when properly read, the great Athenian historian's analysis of war, regimes, and statecraft is far richer and more nuanced than what current international relations theorists can offer for coming to terms with China, Iran, and Russia and for understanding the potential and pitfalls of a democratic nation's response.

* * * * * *

The essays make no effort to consolidate the revisionist drives of China, Iran, and Russia into one overarching model. Each is unique—a fact that makes America's possible responses no less difficult.[2]

As Kagan notes at the start of his chapter, Russia's revisionist behavior is driven by a trio of factors: overturning what Moscow argues are flawed, unfavorable agreements with former Soviet states; revising what it means to be Russia and Russian; and upending the existing international order. Each would be difficult enough to address alone. Combined, they make doing so even more complicated—but also, Kagan writes, just as necessary: "The superficial validity of some of Russia's grievances must not blind us to this reality. The West must find a way to uphold the settlements of the early 1990s, defend the principles of international law and order, and help Russia settle on a new identity within those parameters."

In the case of China, Blumenthal argues that the People's Republic is intent on revising the balance of power in East Asia by returning China to its central place in the regional order, with its past "imperial" rule defining and guiding its efforts to become East Asia's hegemon. Uniquely, Blumenthal writes, "Beijing rules over the world's last remaining multiethnic empire," and the drive to reclaim "lost" territories and prestige and secure that empire both domestically and internationally explains much of Chinese statecraft. But in key respects, Blumenthal notes, "China is in imperial overstretch," and it should be America's strategy to "begin to take advantage of this."

As for Iran, Gerecht posits that, while the Islamic Republic has seen itself as revolutionary since 1979, the broader Islamic agenda has largely "lost its mojo." It has effectively been replaced by a "militant Shi'ite fraternity" designed to give the regime new legitimacy at home and, potentially, a hegemonic position within the Middle East, by playing the Shi'ite card in Iraq, Lebanon, Syria, and Yemen, and among the oppressed Shi'a in Bahrain and Saudi Arabia. But, Gerecht argues, "Iran is a volcano of [internal] contradictions," and Washington would do well to "accentuate those contradictions, especially the century-old Iranian quest for representative government."

In the concluding essay, Walter Russell Mead explains why international relations realists are inclined to define a state's behavior narrowly. As a result, they do not provide an adequate road map for policymakers to use in developing strategies to confront that behavior. "Thucydides was no realist in the modern, American, and academic sense of that term." Today's realism "is a weak and denatured creature, compared to the complex vision of Thucydidean realism, and the costs to analytic coherence are serious."

Certainly, in the limited sense of physical security, none of the three states can honestly claim their own behavior is driven by fear of an American-led invasion. With the end of the Cold War, both Russia and China were more secure than ever and, indeed, remained secure with the significant decline in military spending by the United States and its allies. Even Iran, which from the revolution onward has defined its foreign policy as anti-American, has never been confronted with an American administration determined to overturn its rule. If Tehran faces a possible military strike by its adversaries, it is largely because of the Islamic Republic's own ambition to acquire nuclear weapons.

In Mead's account, in the world of Thucydides, peoples and leaders are moved by a complex mix of interests, fate, and passions, and "no concept could be less congenial" to the Father of History "than the idea that domestic politics and regime type are largely irrelevant to the study of international relations"—which holds true for both autocratic and liberal regimes. In short, it pays to know, in depth, what is driving a state and its leaders; to understand that those drivers cannot be divorced from a country's internal governance; and to realize that, even with such an understanding, unknown and uncontrollable factors will still intercede to shape and limit any strategy.

As important as it is to keep all this in mind, we should not be blind to the one thing that does tie the three revisionist powers together: ambition. None of the three states has been satisfied with an American-led international order, but their ambitions to challenge that order, at least regionally, were initially constrained by their relative lack of economic and military strength, compared to that of the United States and key allies. With the end of the Cold War, that dominance was unprecedented. America and its treaty-bound partners accounted for more than 70 percent of both worldwide military spending and total global gross domestic product (GDP).[3]

Faced with such dominance, China's strategy was "hide our capabilities and bide our time."[4] Similarly, Russia, humiliated by the loss of its superpower status, had to wait until the spike in oil and gas prices unleashed a flood of new revenue to begin to try to reverse the various "capitulations" Yeltsin and Gorbachev had made to Washington and the West out of Soviet, and then Russian, weakness. And while Iran has never concealed its willingness to challenge the United States, its recent assertiveness is undoubtedly tied to the disarray in American Middle East policy, brought about by its multiyear fumbling in Iraq, half-hearted commitment in Afghanistan, and indecision over Syria and the chaos resulting from the Arab Spring. With the combined decline of American and allied economic and military power in recent years, and a general reluctance to use that power assertively, all three states have seized the opportunity to push their revisionist agenda forward.

Policies designed to satiate each of the three countries have not worked. In the cases of Russia and China, American administrations of both political stripes have tried to reset relations and have invited them to join various world forums (such as the World Trade Organization and G20) and generally to recognize their place in the international system. The results have at best been underwhelming. Although some common interests have emerged that have allowed for some cooperation, broader diverging interests and agendas have undermined any real progress toward either Russia or China accepting the responsibilities of having a seat at the table. They have been willing to take advantage of the international order—especially economically—but unwilling to support that order.

China, Iran, and Russia have each been willing participants in the global trading system. But expectations that such participation might help generate internal reforms or at least moderate behavior internationally have gone unmet. If America faces the problem of its own allies free riding in military affairs, it faces an even greater problem of revisionist states free riding by using the open global economic order to generate revenues to fuel their strategic plans.

Until the sanction regime was tightened appreciably during the Bush and Obama years, Iran not only benefited from the open global economic order but also used the massive amount of traffic generated by that order to hide its clandestine efforts to acquire needed elements for its weapons program. President Barack Obama hoped that Tehran—freed from sanctions and with its nuclear prospects supposedly postponed for a decade by the Join Comprehensive Plan of Action—might use the intervening period of lessened tensions to establish a modus vivendi with Saudi Arabia in the region and to reestablish normal trading ties with the rest of the world.[5] Although it is too early to pass final judgment on Obama's strategy, it appears that with sanctions removed, Iran's leadership has accelerated its plans for the region.

The question that needs to be asked is: Do the ambitions of the revisionist powers have recognizable limits? That is, are there concessions to be made, spheres of influence to be accepted, or strategies of appeasement or policies of retrenchment to be adopted that might result in a peaceful status quo? History suggests not. Every gain by a rising power results in a new set of uncertainties within the region and new security interests to be taken into account. As has been noted, Rome conquered the known world with one "defensive" war after another. Success typically opens the door to greater ambition, not less. Building on gains is what rising powers do.

Although the US might for some short time concede greater sway in a region to a revisionist power, the immediate neighbors are not likely to take this advance with equanimity. Either they will take their turn at appeasement, stoking the revisionist power's own views of what it can get away with, or those who can will build up their own military capabilities in response. With Russia and China having nuclear arsenals and Iran potentially on its way to joining them, it is not hard to imagine any number of countries countering with their own weapons programs—programs and capabilities over which the US will have little or no say. A proliferating nuclear arms race is not a recipe for stability.

When a regime's character is factored in, tensions appear virtually inevitable. China, Iran, and Russia all assert a civilizational challenge to the Western liberal democratic order. It is difficult to know how deeply the three countries' general populations hold their leaders' views, but for the leadership in each, ideology is certainly an important source of legitimacy for their non-liberal rule at home.

Coexistence with prosperous, relatively powerful democratic neighbors, whose own relations are largely based on the trust and norms that come from similarity of rule, is a circle hard to square. Even Iran, whose neighborhood is hardly filled with liberal democratic states, must continually strive to keep Iraq, Lebanon, and Syria in a state of chaos, lest a more liberal, majoritarian Shi'ite state emerge and threaten the Islamic Republic's claims to be the only legitimate form of rule for its sect. And the notion that a nation carries a special civilizational role becomes even more important for the leadership to sustain when their ability to meet domestic needs and expectations appears to come up short—a problem Russia, Iran, and, increasingly, China have had.[6]

* * * * * *

Of course, the question is: Why should we care? None of the three states directly threatens the United States. Indeed, arguably, if relations are tense, it is largely because Washington has pushed back against revisionist efforts—often about matters far from our shores and at times over issues for which we have no formal opinion (for example, about who has sovereignty over this or that islet in the South China Sea), no treaty obligation (as with Georgia or Ukraine), or no historical tie (as in Syria).

The answer is that, since World War II's end, Washington has understood that, strategically, Europe, East Asia, and the Middle East are the three most important theaters to the United States and that general peace and global prosperity depend on deterring non-liberal, would-be hegemons from disrupting those regions' stability.[7] If history is any guide, the lesson learned has been that ignoring trouble on those fronts only postpones the difficulty and raises the cost of eventually dealing with it.

Arguably, the Middle East is less important today for the United States, given changing oil and gas markets in the United States. But even so, instability in the region can affect the global energy picture (and hence the world economy), provide openings for terrorism directed at the West, threaten Israel, generate a massive refugee crisis, and produce an arms race that may end with more states attempting to acquire nuclear weapons. American administrations have at various times and for various reasons tried to disentangle the US from the Middle East, but absent US engagement, the region inevitably becomes more anarchic, not less, and generates problems from which Washington has not been able to walk away.

That said, the US faces two major problems in addressing the three revisionist powers in these three key theaters. The first and most obvious problem is that the revisionist powers are there. From a geostrategic perspective, the historical advantage of being separated from Eurasia by two large oceans becomes an obstacle to the US when it comes to creating credible deterrents.

But rather than worry about sustaining a costly forward presence, strategists have offered "offshore balancing" as an alternative. Under this strategy the US will only intervene when one or more powers threaten to gain a hegemonic advantage in a region.

But deciding when to intervene is never easy, since it almost always comes with the prospect of conflict. As a result, democracies in particular are apt to delay intervention until the circumstances are even less advantageous. Moreover, effective and decisive intervention from offshore still requires a military force second to none.[8]

The second major issue is that the costs of deterring another power are clear and felt upfront, but the benefits are unclear and delayed. Arguments in favor of deterrence speculate about what might happen if the US steps back from its forward presence, but until something untoward happens, it remains conjecture. When the public has fresh memories of failing to stop an ambitious power and the country has had to pay for that failure with a costly conflict, it is easier to convince that same public and its representatives that forward-leaning deterrence is the right course. But successful deterrence can also breed complacency—the feeling that the peace and prosperity brought about by that strategy is the natural order of things, not a result of policy decisions made and sustained.[9]

Moreover, it can be difficult to maintain a credible deterrent when the issue at stake—be it territory or some aspect of international law—is important to regional stability but is, at first glance, of only secondary interest to the United States. Such efforts can look even more speculative and costly to the public when, as has been the case in recent years, they have been poorly conducted or inadequately thought through.[10]

* * * * * *

Undoubtedly, the Great Recession of 2008 and the costly, indecisive wars in Afghanistan, Iraq, and Libya have soured large segments of the American public and their representatives on adopting a forward-leaning American strategic posture. With economic problems at home following the recession of 2008, the benefits of such efforts have appeared less than satisfactory.

But this invites two questions: What would the regional and geopolitical situations have been if Washington had not acted? And, as noted already, were the indecisive results a product of strategic overreach, flawed implementation, or a lack of sustained commitment to the task at hand—or some combination of these? The point is not that a forward-leaning posture can prevent costly policy mistakes but rather that one should not simply assume that the larger strategy is to blame for those mistakes.

Nor should we assume that we cannot afford a forward-leaning strategy for Eurasia. Although its primacy is more contested today than in the aftermath of the Cold War, the United States remains the world's only superpower. And while the West—the US and its democratic allies—has seen its overwhelming share of global economic and military power shrink in recent years, it still accounts for some 60 percent of the world's wealth and military spending.[11] Moreover, although the contesting, revisionist powers have the advantage of operating in their own neighborhoods—meaning the US has the more complex and diverse task of responding to challenges far from home—the US has significant, close allies in each region that have begun to spend more on their militaries in the face of the threats posed by China, Iran, and Russia.

Nor have the wars in Iraq and Afghanistan bankrupted the US. At the height of the campaigns, total defense spending (personnel, procurement, operations, etc.) as a percentage of GDP never rose above 5 percent, well below Cold War levels. Today, the base defense budget hovers at 3 percent or less.[12]

In short, if the US and its allies wanted to do more to contest these revisionist powers in the realm of hard military power, they could. It is really a matter of policy choices and priorities.[13]

To take the revisionist challenge seriously requires the American body politic to relearn the value of American leadership in defending the liberal order it largely created after World War II. It requires political leaders to make the case for the benefits that leadership and primacy bring to America. Like an understanding and appreciation of American government itself, this is something that every generation of Americans must (re)learn. Left untaught, it—and the historical memory of its import—will fade.

If there is any "good news" here, it is that recent administrations' decisions to pull back from America's traditional leadership role, to retrench, and to lead from behind have not resulted in a less problematic world.[14] To the contrary, China, Iran, and Russia have all read Washington's reluctance as an opportunity to advance their own plans and have done so in a manner that the American public has noticed.[15] Even absent a major confrontation, American politicians may sense greater instability and greater prospects for conflict. This may lead them to argue the case for reversing course and, with the help of our allies, obtaining the benefits of deterring and containing the revisionist powers. To paraphrase Tocqueville, when it comes to American statecraft, Americans need to relearn the merits of acting on "self-interest rightly understood"—that is, looking not simply to one's immediate interest, but understanding that today's sacrifice may produce a longer-term and more substantial advantage.[16]

But the task at hand is even more complex. China, Iran, and Russia are political models that, at their core, challenge the idea of liberal democracy. Each in its own way sees itself in civilizational opposition to the liberal West, of which the United States is the most prominent exemplar. So the competition cannot be reduced to material and arms. The spirited rejection of liberalism—a seemingly inevitable and repeating byproduct of liberalism's success—needs to be met with a renewed attachment to liberal democracy and the liberal order it fosters.[17]

What sustained America in its fights against Nazi Germany and the Soviet Union was not simply the threat they posed but the view that there was something exceptional about our way of life that deserved to be preserved and spread, where possible. Ronald Reagan's call to "tear down this wall" was not so much a specific policy proposal as the spirited advancement of an agenda around which the US and its democratic allies could rally.

It may be, as President Obama once suggested, that all nations consider themselves exceptional. But by definition they cannot all be exceptional. And more to the point, such relativism undermines the sense of right that must ultimately animate any democratic statecraft that aims to be sustainable over time. In fine, resisting the rise of the revisionist powers requires knowledge of the character of those states, an understanding of the benefits in doing so, a sense of how best to go about the task, and, finally, as Abraham Lincoln might say, a singular dedication to the proposition that liberal democracy is the most just form of government and that its preservation and advancement is good both for us and for the world.

Notes

1. Fareed Zakaria, *The Post-American World: Release 2.0* (New York: W. W. Norton, 2011); Robert Kagan, *The Return of History and the End of Dreams* (New York: Knopf, 2008); and Hal Brands and Eric S. Edelman, *Why Is the World So Unsettled? The End of the Post–Cold War Era and the Crisis of the Global Order*, Center for Strategic and Budgetary Assessments, May 25, 2017, http://csbaonline.org/research/publications/why-is-the-world-so-unsettled-the-end-of-the-post-cold-war-era-and-the-cris. This change in the geopolitical landscape is also reflected in the Trump administration's National Security Strategy: "After being dismissed as a phenomenon of an earlier century, great power competition returned." White House, *National Security Strategy of the United States*, December 2017, 27, https://www.whitehouse.gov/wp-content/uploads/2017/12/NSS-Final-12-18-2017-0905.pdf.

2. Although the Trump administration's National Security Strategy refers to the "revisionist powers of China and Russia," it does not develop that description or note how it might make a difference in American statecraft from seeing China and Russia as just great power competitors. White House, *National Security Strategy of the United States*, 25. Also, Iran is coupled with North Korea under the problem set of rogue regimes. White House, *National Security Strategy of the United States*, 1 and 26. While there is a logic to describing Iran as a rogue regime given its tactics and behavior, there is a case to be made, which Reuel Marc Gerecht does in his essay, that the Iranian leadership's ambitions reach further than destabilizing a region and include establishing a new order for the Middle East.

3. See Stockholm International Peace Research Institute, SIPRI Military Expenditure Database, 2017, https://www.sipri.org/databases/milex; and World Bank, World Development Indicators, 2017, http://data.worldbank.org/data-catalog/world-development-indicators.

4. As outlined in Deng Xiaoping's "24 Character Strategy" of Chinese foreign policy, quoted in US Department of Defense, Office of the Secretary of Defense, *Military Power of the People's Republic of China*, 2007, 6, https://fas.org/nuke/guide/china/dod-2007.pdf.

5. See Jeffrey Goldberg, "The Obama Doctrine," *Atlantic*, April 2016, https://www.theatlantic.com/magazine/archive/2016/04/the-obama-doctrine/471525/.

6. For more information about the economic outlooks of each country, see World Bank Group, *From Recession to Recovery: Russia Economic Report*, May 2017, http://pubdocs.worldbank.org/en/383241495487103815/RER-37-May26-FINAL-with-summary.pdf; World Bank, "Islamic Republic of Iran," 2017, http://pubdocs.worldbank.org/en/847041492266021115/Iran-MEM2017-ENG.pdf; and Dan Blumenthal and Derek M. Scissors, "China's Great Stagnation," *National Interest*, October 17, 2016, http://nationalinterest.org/feature/chinas-great-stagnation-18073.

7. Thomas Wright, *All Measures Short of War: The Contest for the Twenty-First Century and the Future of American Power* (New Haven, CT: Yale University Press, 2017).

8. Stephen G. Brooks, G. John Ikenberry, and William C. Wohlforth, "Lean Forward: In Defense of American Engagement," *Foreign Affairs*, January/February 2013.

9. Robert Kagan, *The Twilight of the Liberal World Order*, Brookings Institution, January 24, 2017, https://www.brookings.edu/research/the-twilight-of-the-liberal-world-order/.

10. Wright, *All Measures Short of War.*

11. See Stockholm International Peace Research Institute, SIPRI Military Expenditure Database; and World Bank, World Development Indicators.

12. See US Office of Management and Budget, "Historical Tables," 2017, https://www.whitehouse.gov/omb/budget/Historicals; and Consolidated Appropriations Act of 2017, Pub. L. No. 115-31.

13. See Marilyn Ware Center for Security Studies, *To Rebuild America's Military*, American Enterprise Institute, October 7, 2015, https://www.aei.org/publication/to-rebuild-americas-military/.

14. Daniel R. Coats, "Worldwide Threat Assessment of the Intelligence Community," Office of the Director of National Intelligence, May 11, 2017, https://www.dni.gov/files/documents/Newsroom/Testimonies/SSCI%20Unclassified%20SFR%20-%20Final.pdf.

15. See, for example, Pew Research Center, *Public Uncertain, Divided over America's Place in the World: Growing Support for Increased Defense Spending*, May 5, 2016, 59, http://www.people-press.org/files/2016/05/05-05-2016-Foreign-policy-APW-release.pdf.

16. See Alexis de Tocqueville, *Democracy in America* (1840), vol. 2, part 2, chap. 8.

17. Abram N. Shulsky, "Liberalism's Beleaguered Victory," *American Interest* 10, no. 1 (August 2014), https://www.the-american-interest.com/2014/08/14/liberalisms-beleaguered-victory/.

1

Russia:
The Kremlin's Many Revisions

FREDERICK W. KAGAN

R ussia is on a collision course with the West. War is not inevitable. Confrontation and conflict are. The sources of hostility are primarily within Russia. They transcend the aims of Vladimir Putin, springing rather from fundamental problems created during the collapse of the Soviet Union. Any Russian leader following Boris Yeltsin would have had to cope with them. Others would have handled them differently, but not necessarily better from the West's perspective or from Russia's.

These problems form inherent and irreducible contradictions in Russia's relationship with the West. Western policy toward Russia must recognize them and accept the reality that Russia will remain hostile to and resentful of the West for some time to come, regardless of Western attempts at conciliation. This conflict is a crypto war, characterized by deception and self-deception, gray zones, and hybrid war, masking Russian crypto-imperialism. We must bring its sources out from the shadows and into the light before we can hope to meet its challenges.

There is no such thing as Weimar Russia. Analogies between Russia today and Germany after World War I minimize the problem now facing the West. German resentment resulted entirely from the harsh peace treaty the victorious Allied powers imposed at Versailles in 1919. Russia was not defeated in a war, nor was any peace treaty imposed. Russia lost its empire in 1991 because of a revolution and nondecision. Soviet Premier Mikhail Gorbachev chose, at the critical moment, to allow the Soviet Union to collapse rather than use force on a massive scale to preserve it. This nondecision shaped the post–Cold War world.

The suddenness of the Soviet collapse was breathtaking and shocking. Soviet republics broke away from the remnants of the union faster than

Moscow could comprehend. Negotiations to settle the myriad complexities of breaking up the largest centralized economy in the world were perfunctory. No process was created to manage the complex citizenship challenges of Russians in the post-Soviet republics or of non-Russians in the Russian Federation. And the Soviet military disintegrated.

Yeltsin immediately faced the determined efforts of the still-powerful Communist Party to restore the Soviet system in some way. He confronted two military attempts to restore Communist rule in 1991 and 1993. With no time or energy to spare from this fight for the survival of Russian democracy, he acquiesced to a new order that did not suit Russia well.

Russia's very identity had collapsed, as the revelations of perestroika undermined the myths and narratives that had undergirded it for seven decades. Yeltsin could do nothing more than establish an identity of freedom and democracy—ideas that seemed increasingly bereft of value as the Russian economy collapsed in the 1990s.

Putin took power in 2000, determined to address these crises. He is redefining Russian identity in terms the tsars used in the 19th century—Russian Orthodoxy, nationalism, and strong government. (They called it autocracy, but he does not.) He claims the right to renegotiate the bad deals Russia made with the post-Soviet states, by force if necessary. He cites the plight of ethnic Russians in the new republics as justification for eroding or even erasing the sovereignty of those states. He seeks to restore Russia to the global eminence it had as the Soviet Union, by reestablishing its positions in the Middle East, Asia, and Africa. He stokes conflict with the West to distract it from these endeavors, even as he blames the West for inventing the hostility he has created.

The West cannot appease its way out of this crypto war. Putin requires conflict to justify his rule at home and his actions in the territory of the former Soviet Union. But Western appeasement cannot address problems that spring from deep within Russia itself. Putin is encouraging Russians to believe that they must regain suzerainty over their former empire, that they must weaken and fragment the West, that they must cut the United States down to size, and that the West will oppose them implacably in all these endeavors. Appeasement can only draw him into further demands, since he cannot allow the hostility to wane.

Russia's Revisionist Roots

Russia is a revisionist state seeking to reclaim a lost empire. Its approach is idiosyncratic, reflecting its unique situation after the end of the Cold War. Russia was not actually defeated in that war. It chose to give up its empire rather than fight for it. It set new boundaries and relationships with its newly independent neighbors of its own accord. There was never any Versailles Treaty, and so there can be no Weimar Russia. Russian revisionism is thus an attempt to renegotiate by force a peace that it freely made.

A trinity of revisionist drives governs Russian behavior. First, Moscow seeks to revise its agreements with the other former Soviet states. Second, it is revising the very meaning of "Russia" and "Russian." Third, President Vladimir Putin seeks to revise the international order fundamentally. These drives are interwoven, but they exist independently. Their mutual interactions pose an almost intractable problem for American and European policymakers.

Status quo powers can hope to resist a state seeking only to revise the international order by demonstrating to it the impossibility of succeeding in that aim. Such attempts often lead to war, when the revisionist power is strong and determined enough (Germany before World War I, for example) or the status quo powers are weak or indecisive (as in the 1930s). The requirement is relatively simple to articulate, if not to meet. But the West's task in dealing with Russia today is not so simple.

Post-Soviet Russia must find a new identity and come to terms with the agreements that set its post–Cold War boundaries and relations with its new neighbors. The Russian nationalist narrative holds that those agreements were foolish, mistaken, and forced on Russia and have not been honored by Russia's neighbors. There is some truth in that narrative.

Internal conditions in Russia, as the Soviet Union fell, drove Boris Yeltsin to advance and then accept a series of deals that did not serve Russia's interests in the long term. The press of time and circumstances precluded careful deliberations and the development of any meaningful plans to address the inevitable complexities of breaking up a vast, centralized, polyglot empire. The terms of the post–Cold War settlement changed dramatically to Moscow's detriment, as the Soviet empire collapsed and the US position evolved from assurances that NATO would not expand eastward to the full incorporation of East Germany and then the Baltic States into the alliance.[1] Russian unhappiness with all these events is understandable.

A student of Russian history can even empathize with Russia's complaints. But comprehension and empathy are not agreement or approval. The hard fact is that international law and centuries-old custom require Russia to live within the terms of the agreements it made or renegotiate them peacefully and on equal terms with its partners. Russia's recent use of force and coercion to compel the former Soviet states to concede to its demands is unjustifiable and anathema to a healthy and peaceful world order. The international community must resist rather than condone—let alone encourage—it.

The American and European need to resist Russia's forceful reconquest is relatively easy to articulate and defend, but less easy to undertake. The challenge lies in finding the correct response to the first two revisionist drives—renegotiating the Cold War–ending agreements and searching for a new (or old) Russian identity. The temptation here is to think that the West can conciliate Moscow in some way that will lead to a mutually acceptable agreement. That temptation above all must be resisted. The interaction of all three of Russia's revisionisms makes such an agreement impossible on any terms the West could accept.

The superficial validity of some of Russia's grievances must not blind us to this reality. The West must find a way to uphold the settlements of the early 1990s, defend the principles of international law and order, and help Russia settle on a new identity within those parameters.

The Internal-International Divide

The West did not defeat Russia at the end of the Cold War. Rather, the Soviet Union imploded in a complex revolution that ended the conflict almost as an aside.[2] Nor did the West impose a settlement on Russia. Negotiations among the former Soviet states decided the most important elements of the post–Cold War world for Russia.

The resulting settlement is what Putin seeks to revise in the first instance. His problem is thus not initially with the victorious powers, but rather with the constituent parts of the Soviet Union. He views this problem as an internal one. Russia made a number of mistakes in the course of that settlement, which we will consider presently. The Russians feel that other Soviet states also violated their commitments to Russia.[3] Putin believes that Russia therefore has a right to revise the settlement, both to correct the mistakes and to hold its former partners to their promises.[4]

This poses a problem for the rest of the international community. The US, NATO, and their partners did not decree the resolution of the Cold War, but they did guarantee elements of it by recognizing the former Soviet states as independent countries.[5] They did not guarantee that those newly independent states would abide by promises made to Russia in the course of negotiations, since those were bilateral issues on the whole. And they certainly did not guarantee Russia any right to enforce those promises, still less to revise the series of agreements of which they were a part.

The West's view is and must be that the settlement of the Cold War became an international matter rather than an internal one when the new states received formal recognition. This view is incompatible with Putin's, and the differences are likely irreducible.

The Fall of the Soviet Union

The details of the USSR's collapse are extremely hazy to most Westerners and increasingly so to many Russians. The Soviet state's collapse and the emergence of 15 independent countries seem inevitable in retrospect, as most historical events do. It may, indeed, have been inevitable once certain key decisions were made—but there was nothing inevitable about those decisions.

One thing is clear: No decision to break up the Soviet Union was made, nor was there ever a plan for how to do so. The Soviet collapse was the cumulative result of decisions and events occurring simultaneously and over time in many places, often without Moscow's participation and sometimes without its knowledge. A nondecision set it all in motion.

As the Warsaw Pact countries began to drift away and independence movements arose and flourished in various parts of the Soviet Union, Soviet leader Mikhail Gorbachev decided against using force to retain the Soviet empire. "A witness recalls Gorbachev saying in the late 1980s: 'We are told that we should pound the fist on the table,' and the general secretary clenched his hand in fist to 'show how it is done.' 'Generally speaking,' continued Gorbachev, 'it could be done. But one does not feel like it.'"[6] Gorbachev did not desire to allow the Soviet Union to fall, but he was unwilling to restore Stalinist repression to prevent it.

As it became clear that the center would not hold, Gorbachev and then Yeltsin tried to negotiate various arrangements with the individual Soviet Socialist Republics to retain some kind of decentralized federal system with Moscow at its heart. The hopelessness of this undertaking was by no means apparent to everyone involved. Russia's leaders quickly resigned themselves to losing the Baltic States and possibly some of the Caucasian republics. Those peoples had long histories of independent statehood and relatively strong national identities, despite the efforts of the Russian Empire and the Soviet Union to Russify or Sovietize them.

The shocks came when Ukraine, Belarus, and the five Central Asian republics declared their independence and refused to join any meaningful federal system. Ukraine and Belarus had never really been independent states before, and their national identities were relatively recent and complex.[7] The peoples of Central Asia had long traditions of independence before the Russian conquests of their lands—but not as states in anything like their current configurations. Stalin had invented their borders during and after the Soviet reconquest in the 1920s. He drew the lines deliberately to create tension and conflict among the republics rather than to encapsulate peoples with common identities.[8] None of these republics seemed predestined to choose a path of total independence from Moscow, and Russia's leaders were stunned when they all did.[9]

The sudden and unexpected nature of their decisions created a real dilemma for the ethnic Russians living in those lands. As Putin said, "The collapse of the Soviet Union was a major geopolitical disaster of the century. As for the Russian nation, it became a genuine drama. Tens of millions of our co-citizens and compatriots found themselves outside Russian territory. Moreover the epidemic of disintegration infected Russia itself."[10] Russians, he added later, "went to bed in one country and awoke in different ones, overnight becoming ethnic minorities in former Union republics, while the Russian nation became one of the biggest, if not the biggest ethnic group in the world to be divided by borders."[11]

No plans for ensuring their rights as newfound minorities in newly formed states had been developed. Several of the former Soviet republics promised to protect those rights, but many promises were not kept.[12] Ethnic Russians in the Baltic republics and Moldova were discriminated against, denied citizenship and passports, and otherwise marginalized.[13] Many emigrated to Russia, but many remained.

This phenomenon is common to the process of decolonization, which frequently leaves the citizens of the colonial power in difficult circumstances in the newly independent states. In cases in which decolonization resulted from a deliberate policy act by the colonial power, citizens often had warning, time, and sometimes assistance. Sometimes they were guaranteed some protections by the newly independent regime. The process was always messy, frustrating, and disappointing for all sides. But it was, at least, often an actual process.

There was no such process in the decolonization of the Soviet empire, nor is the parallel entirely fair to the Russians in the newly independent states. Russians had not colonized Ukraine or Belarus in any meaningful way—they had been there for as long as the current Slavic inhabitants had. It is fairer to say that some in Ukraine and Belarus evolved out of Russianness into new identities while others did not.[14] Similar complexities attended the historical status of Russian minorities in the other republics. All of which is to say that those concerned with the well-being of ethnic Russians had reason to be highly dissatisfied with the way their conationalists were treated during the breakup of the Soviet Union and to regard the manner of that breakup as badly planned and unfair.[15]

This perception of unfairness and dishonesty in the way the new states emerged from the Soviet Union embittered Russian leaders at the time. Yeltsin resented it, and his Communist and nationalist political opponents resented it still more. The Russian Federation passed various laws in the 1990s extending rights to Russian minorities in the newly independent states. Russian policy documents claimed the right to protect those minorities long before Putin was a national figure.[16] The desire to revise this aspect of the Cold War "settlement" has deep roots in the Russian polity that precedes and transcends Putin's current machinations. They form a part of a fundamental revisionist drive that any Russian leader is likely to feel—although not necessarily to heed.

National Security and the New States

The collapse of the Soviet Union was unique in still another way. The "colonial" power, to use that historical analogy, lost political control and influence before it had withdrawn its military power—before, even, there was any agreement about how it would do so.

The problem was threefold. First, the Soviet military followed the age-old imperial practice of deploying conscripts in mixed units, generally far from their homelands. There was no easy way, therefore, to break it up along the new political lines.

Second, Soviet strategic systems, especially nuclear systems, were deployed throughout the former USSR. The nuclear systems were in Belarus, Kazakhstan, and Ukraine, in addition to Russia. Both Moscow and the international community were determined to ensure that one nuclear power emerged from the ruins, not four. The Black Sea Fleet was based at Sevastopol, which was suddenly Ukrainian territory.

Third, the Soviet military industry had been spread throughout the entire Soviet empire but was concentrated in Kazakhstan, Russia, and Ukraine. The question of what was to become of the components outside Russia had many thorny consequences.[17]

All these issues warranted long negotiations and studies with valid arguments on all sides. They were instead decided quickly, in some cases almost en passant, without any general agreement on principles, and in the context of chaos and near civil war in Russia itself. Russia could claim the right to all the Soviet Union's nuclear weapons, the Black Sea Fleet, and other strategic assets only on grounds of pragmatism or extreme ethnocentrism. Representatives of all the Soviet republics were involved in building those systems; resources from all the republics were used to fund them.

The case for sharing them among the various newly independent states was not weak, at least from a moral perspective. But Moscow refused to countenance independent nuclear states on its borders, and the West was equally horrified by the prospect of four different states armed with intercontinental ballistic missiles.

Even so, negotiations to establish the Russian monopoly on nuclear weapons were not easy, with Ukraine holding out until 1994.[18] The Black Sea Fleet question was more difficult for Moscow. A weak and preoccupied

Yeltsin agreed to split the Black Sea Fleet with Ukraine, acknowledge Ukraine's territorial ownership of the Russian part of the fleet's base, and enter into a limited lease for it.[19]

Russia flat-out lost on the question of military industry. Factories in Ukraine and elsewhere continued to function (to the extent that any post-Soviet industry functioned), now owned by Ukrainian oligarchs and producing weapons for the benefit of Ukraine. Those factories, once just a part of the Soviet weapons production and export system, suddenly became competitors in one of the new Russian state's only significant exports. Moreover, the Russian defense industry continued to rely on components produced in some of these factories. The full unwinding of this artificial disruption in a previously coherent supply chain only began with the 2014 Russo-Ukrainian conflict, and it is not yet complete.

All these issues were international matters by the time they were resolved, since the component Soviet republics were declared and recognized independent states by the end of 1991 and had seats in the UN General Assembly by July 1992. The Russo-Ukrainian agreement regarding Sevastopol and the Black Sea Fleet was an international agreement, not an internal matter.[20] The US was a party to the agreement regarding Ukraine's nuclear arsenal. In reality, and for the West, any changes to these agreements must result from voluntary diplomatic undertakings between equal states. Yeltsin also regarded them as such perforce—he negotiated them with sovereign governments. Anyone who believes in upholding and defending international law can take no other view.

But Putin's perspective is different. The complexities regarding the disposition of Sevastopol, Crimea, the Black Sea Fleet, and so on arose from internal Soviet decisions. Had anyone thought that those decisions would lead to outcomes that would be internationally recognized and permanent, he argues, they would not have been made in that way. He says of Nikita Khrushchev's decision to transfer Crimea to Ukraine, "This decision was treated as a formality of sorts because the territory was transferred within the boundaries of a single state. Back then, it was impossible to imagine that Ukraine and Russia may split up and become two separate states."[21] Russia had an implicit right, he suggests, to revise those internal decisions before they became internationalized.

Thus Putin unilaterally renounced Russia's agreements regarding the Black Sea Fleet division and the use of Sevastopol, shortly after seizing the Crimean Peninsula and almost without comment.[22] According to him, Crimean issues have always been internal Russian matters, and so they should remain.

The argument here falls short of asserting Moscow's right to suzerainty, let alone sovereignty, over the whole territory of the former Soviet Union. It is a narrower revisionist argument, focused on the way decisions were made before and during the collapse of the USSR and the rights of the post-Soviet states (especially Russia) to revise those decisions ex post facto.

This is not to say that Putin's sole aim is to reconstitute the Soviet state or the Russian Empire. We will consider that issue presently. It is, rather, to isolate a problem that is both more limited and more fundamental—namely, that the Russian view is irreconcilable with the Western view, even putting all questions of neo-imperialism aside. And it has nothing in common with Weimar, still less Hitlerite Germany.[23]

Neo-Imperialism

Putin does have a neo-imperial agenda, however, above and beyond—yet interconnected with—this issue. This agenda arises from a second revisionism that likewise had no parallel in postwar Germany. Putin feels the need to revise Russia's identity and national narrative. This need arises from two grounds. First, the collapse of the Soviet empire required it. Second, the pain of the introspection of perestroika (the reforms Mikhail Gorbachev undertook in the late 1980s that led to the collapse of the Soviet Union) is soothed by it.

Russian identity had become so closely enmeshed with the Soviet Union by the end of World War II that it was hardly possible to disentangle the two. The collapse of the USSR inevitably led to a massive identity crisis for Russia. Many of the newly independent post-Soviet states seemed eager and happy to embrace historical and ethnic identities long suppressed by the Soviets and the imperial Russians before them, aggravating that identity crisis. Their emerging identities thus came at Russia's expense, even as Russia's own identity crumbled. Something had to be done.

Yeltsin was not able to address the identity crisis, nor did he really try. His mission was to move Russia from a Soviet to a post-Soviet mind-set.

He spent virtually his entire reign in that fight, which he nearly lost several times. He accomplished it, really, only after the 1996 presidential election, in which he defeated the Communist candidate and thereby started the final collapse of the Communist Party. In the end, he managed to make Russians into post-Soviets—but not into new Russians.[24]

Putin took that problem in hand and made it part of his focus. What was Russia now? It was no longer post-Soviet. It had to be something new—or, rather, old. The definition of Russia inevitably reached back into history, as national identities always do. But to which history? This was no small question in the 1990s because perestroika had fundamentally revised Russians' understanding of their own Soviet history, very much for the worse.

Perestroika

Distorting and obfuscating events and history was a hallmark of the Soviet regime. It concealed the extent of its crimes from its own people with remarkable success. Russians knew bad things had happened during Stalin's purges and collectivization, but they did not know how bad or how extensive those things were. Soviet history concealed that Stalin miscalculated terribly in 1939–41, leaving the country open to an attack that surprised him—an attack for which he could have been prepared.[25] Soviet citizens were taught, rather, that World War II—known as the Great Patriotic War—was a bitter but glorious moment in their history, imposed by Hitler, who was driven by the Western states in his attempt to destroy the Soviet Union.[26]

Perestroika transformed Russians' fundamental understanding of their Soviet past. Suddenly they were presented with the full panoply of the horrors of collectivization and realized the actual death toll for the first time. They learned that Stalin had been a fool and that the Great Patriotic War could have cost the Soviets infinitely less than it did. They gained a detailed knowledge of all the evil things the Soviet system had done to its own people, deeply tarnishing what they had believed to be a glorious past.

Many Soviet citizens suffered a sort of collective survivor's guilt as well. They learned that they had been victimized far more than they had ever understood and that they themselves were partly to blame for the even greater horrors inflicted on those who perished, because those who lived and participated in the system facilitated the crimes and benefited from them to some extent.

They prided themselves on their honesty, noting that they were making their own accounting of their government's past deeds, of their own will. They were not forced to do so by victorious powers, as Germany and Japan had been. But the pride was somber, felt only by some, and did not mitigate the psychological damage done by the destruction of a historical narrative of which they had been proud.

The revision of perestroika's version of history began quickly. Yeltsin's political opponents on both the left and the right began attacking it early in the 1990s. The Communists, led by Gennady Zyuganov, argued for the Soviet system's achievements. Their arguments became more salient and convincing as the post-Soviet system led to initial dramatic decreases in most Russians' quality of life. Nostalgia for the old regime grew rapidly, propelling the Communists to a sustained third of the popular vote and a dominant role in the legislature throughout the 1990s.[27]

But that third of the vote seemed to be a hard ceiling, and nostalgia for communism was not a substitute for a new identity. The right-wing party of Vladimir Zhirinovskii began the process of constructing that identity. Largely accepting the perestroika narrative of Soviet failures, Russian nationalists opened the aperture on Russia's history. They reclaimed the notion of Russia's unique place and role in the world and tried to assume the mantle of Russian imperialism in a positive light. They began to speak of pre-Soviet heroes, going back many hundreds of years, while trying to get Russian citizens to think of themselves as descendants of Riurik, Ivan the Terrible, and Peter the Great.

Zhirinovskii failed to garner significant electoral support, however. His party, and the Communists even more, also began to embrace the darker sides of Russian history. They were in full cry for atavistic anti-Semitism of the sort that had fueled the tsarist pogroms and Soviet repression of Jews by the end of the decade. Some embraced fascism openly, sporting neo-Nazi symbols and even praising Hitler.

Both the nationalists and the Communists were trounced at the polls. Zyuganov lost the 1996 presidential election to Yeltsin despite entering the contest with an overwhelming lead.[28] Communist dominance of the legislature evaporated in the 1999 legislative elections, while the always-weak nationalist block collapsed almost entirely. In the 2000 presidential election Putin crushed Zyuganov and the others, winning in the first round by over 20 percentage points.[29] These parties thus failed to create a new identity for Russia, although they sowed some seeds.[30]

Putin tended those seeds and harvested their fruit from the first days of his administration. He harked back to the days of Riurik, the legendary founder of Russia, in his "Open Letter to Voters" in February 2000: "Our land is rich, only there is no order in it."[31] Medieval chronicles report that the ancient Slavs wrote this to the Viking Riurik, whose people were called the Rus, in 860–62.[32] Putin omitted the last part of the sentence, however: "Come to rule and reign over us." So Riurik moved to Novgorod and created the first Russian state and people. It was a remarkably and uncharacteristically nuanced and deft bit of rhetoric to mark the start of a coherent effort to redefine Russia as the inheritor of more than a millennium of expansion and triumph. Did Putin mean slyly to cast himself in the role of Riurik, father of the Russians?

Who are the Russians, then, according to Putin? They are an ancient Slavic people, descended from the Rus, who inhabited the land from Ukraine to Finland. They have been Christian for more than a millennium, following Vladimir the Great's conversion in 988. When the Christian church split in 1054, Russians followed the Eastern Orthodox rite and its leader, the Patriarch of Constantinople. When the Ottomans conquered Constantinople, the Russians became the principal inheritors and defenders of the Orthodox tradition. An apologist for Ivan the Terrible, in fact, identified Moscow as the "third Rome," Constantinople's successor as the leading city of all Christians.[33]

The Russians also inherited the glory, traditions, and patrimony of the Kievan Rus, principalities of which Kiev was, naturally, the center. Putin noted that Ukraine and Russia "are not simply close neighbours but . . . we are one people. Kiev is the mother of Russian cities. Ancient Rus is our common source and we cannot live without each other."[34] The Russians fought the Mongol invasions and thus claim to be defenders of Europe and Christianity against the Asian hordes (although Kiev was destroyed and Moscow became a Mongol client for a time).

They are also the heirs to Peter the Great, who brought Western ideas into Russia while conquering Western lands. Peter defeated Sweden in the early 18th century to "plant a foot firmly on the [Baltic] Sea" and "break through a window into Europe," in Pushkin's words.[35] Peter modernized Russia and set it on the path to becoming a great power.

Russia's Europeanness is essential to Putin: "Above all else Russia was, is and will, of course, be a major European power. . . . For three centuries, we—together with the other European nations—passed hand in hand through reforms of Enlightenment, the difficulties of emerging parliamentarism, municipal and judicial branches, and the establishment of similar legal systems. . . . We did this together, sometimes behind and sometimes ahead of European standards."[36]

Aleksandr I revived Russian messianism following Napoleon's 1812 invasion. Russian armies fighting under the icons of Orthodoxy drove the French all the way back to Paris, freeing Europe from the yoke of tyranny in the first Patriotic War. His successors crafted the guiding doctrines of the late Russian Empire, based on the principles of Orthodoxy, nationalism, and autocracy.

Putin embraces the 20th-century version of that messianism, noting that the celebration of the end of World War II in Europe (Victory Day) "can [be] justly called the day of civilisation's triumph over fascism. Our common victory enabled us to defend the principles of freedom, independence, and equality between all peoples and nations. . . . [Russian soldiers] saved the world from an ideology of hatred and tyranny." "Also certain is that Russia should continue its civilising mission on the Eurasian continent. This mission consists in ensuring that democratic values, combined with national interests, enrich and strengthen our historic community."[37]

Russians are above all, however, members of an ancient nation-state. The greatest heroes of pre-Romanov (that is, pre–17th century) history are those who participated in what is known as the gathering of the Russian lands.[38] All territories inhabited by Russians were part of a single state by the end of the 16th century. They remained part of a single state until 1991, apart from brief periods of disorder. Russian nationalists believe they should be part of a single state or, rather, of a single polity that includes, in the odd phrase of the tsars, "all the Russias."[39]

The collapse of the Soviet Union destroyed the unity of Russian lands, undoing centuries of conquest and then imperial retention. Russian nationalists will find it hard, perhaps impossible, to reconcile themselves to the loss of those lands, at least as long as they rely on historical concepts to define Russia's identity.

Post-Soviet Russia is most like Weimar Germany in this respect. Nationalists regard the truncation of the Russian state as unnatural and artificial. They seek to reunify lands that were historically whole. Putin himself compared Russia to Germany at the end of the Cold War (eschewing deliberately, no doubt, any hint of Weimar Russia). He noted, falsely, that Russia had supported Germany's quest for reunification in 1990 and asked Germany to do the same for Russia in return. He was speaking at that moment only of Crimea, but there is no reason to distinguish Crimea from any of the other "traditionally" or "historically" Russian lands.[40]

The Russian national identity thus defined is therefore inevitably revisionist and neo-imperialist. It must seek to reestablish Moscow's control over at least the lands inhabited by Russians, if not over all the lands ever governed by Russia.

But this neo-imperialism is forced to be crypto-imperialism, at least for the moment, by the fact that Russia itself acknowledged and accepted the loss of these lands. The absence of a Versailles Treaty imposed and enforced by victorious foreign powers greatly complicates Putin's efforts to lay claim to the former Soviet republics. He can—and does—complain about the way in which the devolution of the Soviet empire proceeded, but he has found it impossible thus far to justify simply demanding the reversal of that process.

The crypto nature of this imperialism is reflected in the way Putin has been pursuing it. He is unable to blame everything on foreign powers and demand that they redress his grievances; he relies instead on established arguments for Russia's rights to protect Russians in the former Soviet republics. This is not simply a matter of "gray zone" warfare. It also reflects the challenges he faces in the ideological basis of his attempt to regather the Russian lands.

And the problem is not simply a matter of conflict with the West. As Leon Aron and others have argued eloquently—and Russians argued at the time—there is a correlation between Russian (or Soviet) imperialism and autocracy at home.[41] Faced with the choice between domestic liberty and retaining the empire, Russian leaders and people chose the former every time in the 1990s. Putin may wish it had been otherwise and is making the opposite choices today. But he operates in a world of narratives not just made up of his own devising.

The narrative of Russian liberty is important, and it does not easily coincide with a neo-imperial narrative baldly expressed. The crypto-imperialism that relies on the oppression of Russians and seemingly nit-picking arguments about promises not kept is therefore aimed as much at keeping elements of the Russian population on board as it is at facilitating hybrid warfare against the West.[42]

It also handles another challenge Putin inherited from the 1990s—namely, the feeling that Russia should focus on making itself strong and not waste its energy on struggles beyond its borders. The rhetorical and ideological impossibility of simply making the leap back to saying that the Soviet borders are Russia's actual borders makes it harder for Putin to argue that any and all Russian activities in former Soviet states are worthy expenditures of Russian blood and treasure. This is yet another reason for the cryptic nature of his neo-imperial drive.

There are outright Russian nationalists in Russia, to be sure, and in large numbers. They make up a growing portion of Putin's electoral base, in fact.[43] They are not numerous enough to win Putin elections, however, particularly when Russia's economy is doing so poorly.

Putin faces several options in the run-up to the next round of presidential elections in 2018. He can try to turn the economy around and regain enough popularity to win without egregiously rigging the voting. He can try to develop enough support to win based on noneconomic issues such as patriotism and nationalism. He can try just to rig the voting. Or he can dispense with the forms of representative government by suspending elections temporarily or permanently.

He is least likely to choose the last path, which would lead to international denunciation and isolation and also alienate a large segment of the population. It would also destroy his regime's ideological basis and force him to develop an entirely new one. He is instead working on the first three simultaneously.

But he faces a conundrum in this effort. Attempts to stir up atavistic nationalism rely on identifying enemies abroad and confronting them, at least in Putin's approach. Putin and his attack dogs thus vilify the pro-Western post-Soviet states and justify military threats and actions against them. They also rely heavily on a narrative of confrontation and enmity toward the Western powers, particularly the US. They thus pursue the traditional paths of Soviet and imperial Russian argumentation that define Russia as a strong and righteous power encircled by malign and hostile states, against which it must mobilize to defend itself.[44]

That narrative, however, runs athwart the most direct path to improving Russia's economy in the short run—namely, sanctions relief. The Russian economy suffers many deep structural problems, as Putin has long noted and lamented. Its transition from the Soviet centralized and state-owned economy has been partial and fraught. Privatization placed vast enterprises in the hands of oligarchs. Inadequate legal structures and poor tax policies—and even poorer mechanisms for collecting taxes—failed to woo sufficient international investment even before the sanctions began, following the invasion of Crimea in 2014. The Russian economy was and remains in the grip of robber barons who owe their positions to Putin. Thus, it never moved past the status of rentier state based primarily on mineral wealth, despite the skill of its educated classes.

There are no quick fixes for this problem, as Putin discovered in his first 14 years in power (as president and prime minister). The economy did well enough to satisfy many Russians when oil prices and oil-indexed gas prices were high. The collapse of the oil market, however, put Russia in a terrible position from which it would not easily have recovered. The imposition of strong sanctions in 2014 and 2015 pushed it over the edge.

Putin recognizes all this and focuses on the one aspect of the problem that could change and improve the economy quickly—relaxing or ending sanctions. Yet he faces a dilemma. He needs to pursue confrontational policies to support nationalism and advance the crypto-imperialism required to regather the Russian lands. But those policies make it hard for him to concede to Western demands for sanctions relief.

I am deliberately setting aside here the questions that arise from attempts to psychoanalyze Putin. Various statements in his pseudo-autobiography and as president suggest that he would not be inclined to resolve a problem by backing down in any case.[45] He has, however, shown a strong sense of pragmatism when serious issues were on the line, as, for example, in his response to Turkey shooting down a Russian fighter aircraft. Efforts to read his soul are too weak a basis on which to formulate policy when there are alternatives. The structural problems facing him, were he to seek sanctions relief through compromise, make it unnecessary to guess how he would make decisions in a vacuum.

Putin has therefore chosen other paths to achieve sanctions relief. He is using bribery in various forms to seduce one or more EU states, in hopes that they might veto a sanctions extension. He is actively working to weaken the EU in general by supporting euroskeptic parties. He is ostentatiously flexing his military muscles in an attempt to coerce European states to concede. And he is rheostating the conflict in Ukraine to gain leverage in sanctions negotiations.

These efforts have not yet eroded the sanctions. They have, however, steadily shifted the character of the intra-European discussion about sanctions in Putin's favor. It is unlikely that the sanctions will survive, absent a significant change in the situation.[46]

Russia's attempt to break the post-Crimea sanctions is not a form of direct revisionism, since the sanctions themselves are a new phenomenon. These efforts are, rather, an attempt to mitigate the effects of revisionist policies without abandoning or moderating those policies. They weave nicely into a larger undertaking to revise the international order fundamentally.

Revising the World Order

Putin rejects the post–Cold War international structure fundamentally. He insists that it is unraveling, which he views as good. He aims to assist with that unraveling and claims to seek a new order that is more peaceful, stable, and just. He is in this respect a revisionist of the most traditional sort.

Russia's fall from superpower status in 1991 shocked its leaders and probably many of its people. The shock came not merely from the fact that the Soviet Union had been a superpower. The Russian Empire had regarded itself as more than a great power since the early 19th century at least. Aleksandr I's defeat of Napoleon established Russia as the dominant power in Eastern Europe. Prussia and Austria fell into nearly vassal status after 1807 and remained there for many decades.

Nicholas I, Aleksandr's successor, was known as the gendarme of Europe and embraced the role. He was readying an army to suppress the Belgian Revolution in 1830, when a revolt in his own Polish lands diverted him. He did send a large force to quell the Hungarian uprising against Austria in 1849. His defeat in the Crimean War (1853–56) drove his son, Aleksandr II, to focus on massive internal reforms, including emancipating the serfs in 1861.

Russia's distraction facilitated the work of Otto von Bismarck and Helmuth von Moltke the Elder to unify Germany, creating a strong rival on Russia's western frontier in 1871 for the first time in more than a century. Even so, Russia remained much stronger than both Austria (now Austria-Hungary) and the declining Ottoman Empire. Its pretensions to first-rank great-power status remained until the empire's collapse in 1917.

Any Russian nationalist contemplating Russia's traditional role in the international system, therefore, would expect Russia to be among the most powerful and respected states—and to be treated accordingly. The sudden Soviet collapse, however, stripped Russia of almost any right to such pretentions. Moscow lost a sizable portion of its territory and nearly half of its population almost overnight. Its economy collapsed, as did its military. It became mired in domestic struggles that nearly destroyed it, including two failed coup attempts in the 1990s.

Russia effectively vanished from the world scene as any sort of meaningful actor for almost a decade. Only Russia's nuclear arsenal required other states to treat it as anything other than a weak, if large, regional state with little ability to affect its neighbors.

Russia had suffered hard times in the past. Succession struggles in the mid-18th century periodically drove Russia inward. Tsar Paul's defeat at the hands of Napoleon in 1799 caused a retreat from European power politics for a few years. We have considered the aftermath of the Crimean War. Russia's loss to Japan in 1905 generated a brief revolution and a similar withdrawal and loss of face and influence. But Russia always returned to first-rank status after such setbacks. Putin's desire to repeat that experience in the current environment is not surprising.

The post–Cold War international order posed a novel problem for a Russia seeking to "rise from its knees," as Putin likes to say, and rejoin the ranks of the great powers: American global dominance.[47] Never before in modern history had a single state amassed such a disproportionate influence over the entire world. Louis XVI, Napoleon, and Hitler had dreamed of a universal empire and undertaken to achieve it, but all had failed. The US was not an empire, but it had achieved global preponderance of which these historical figures could only dream. There was thus no body of great powers that Russia could rejoin after getting its house in order. There was one superpower, whose strength Russia could not hope to match in any time frame Putin was willing to accept.

The European states could have counterbalanced the US had they been sufficiently unified and willing to oppose Washington. But the European project was only just getting underway in the 1990s, and the reunification of Germany focused Europe inward for a time. The US, in Putin's view, seized the opportunity to consolidate its control over Europe by strengthening and empowering NATO, thereby subjugating Europe to America's will. It proclaimed itself the "indispensable nation" and spoke of "unipolarity," suggesting that the US was all too well aware of its ability to establish a protracted global hegemony and its desire to do so.[48]

Yeltsin allowed this phenomenon to proceed unchecked. Indeed, he acquiesced to it, through both action and inaction. Russia did nothing when a US-led European coalition invaded the former Yugoslavia (as Putin saw it), supporting ethno-religious separatism at the expense of Russia's favored South Slavic client, Serbia. Yeltsin only weakly protested expanding NATO into first the Warsaw Pact countries and then onto the territory of the former Soviet Union itself. The expansion seemed to Russians to violate agreements Moscow thought it had secured as the USSR fell apart, but Yeltsin signed an agreement with NATO accepting both the expansion and an observer status for Russia in America's hegemonic alliance.[49]

Putin was determined to do better than Yeltsin at standing up to the US. American hegemony was intolerable in itself because it deprived Russia of its rightful role in the world. It was also the primary obstacle to Putin's efforts to restore Russia's identity and regather the Russian lands.

It was also, he believed, illegal. The US and its allies rewrote international law to suit themselves. They had no right to involve themselves in Kosovo in 1999. Rather than obtaining a UN Security Council resolution that would have given them such a right, they asserted a doctrine that Putin found not only illegal but also extremely threatening—that the decision by NATO to act was enough to give international legitimacy to an invasion of a sovereign state. They then supported Kosovo's unilateral declaration of independence. Putin constantly condemns both actions but also cites them as precedential justifications for his own undertakings in the former Soviet lands.[50]

Putin has steadily added to the list of supposed violations of international laws and norms by the US and NATO over time. He condemned the Iraq invasion in 2003, of course.[51] He bitterly assailed the NATO-led operation that removed Muammar Qaddafi from power in Libya in 2011.[52] He felt particularly betrayed in that instance because NATO seized on a UN Security Council resolution that Putin had specifically crafted to avoid giving it the right to take direct military action. He viewed the imposition of sanctions on his personal allies and then on sections of the Russian economy after the Crimean invasion as evidence of America's determination to use its economic power to subjugate Russia and any other state that might oppose it.[53]

He is committed to cutting the US back down to size, weakening or fragmenting NATO, and ensuring that the EU cannot act as a concerted bloc against him, at a minimum to reverse this deplorable situation. He has made common cause with the other states that resent American and European domination, particularly Iran and China. His aim is to re-create a world order in which Russia is respected as much or more than the US, has regained its traditional preponderant influence in Europe, has reestablished itself as a major player in the Middle East and Asia, and wields veto power over any actions other states might take beyond their borders or to Russia's detriment.

He regards his argument against American hegemony as self-demonstrating. American actions have not only been illegal—they have been devastatingly ineffective and, indeed, counterproductive. US interference in Afghanistan in the 1980s created the al Qaeda threat, he argues, by supporting the radical Islamist factions of the mujahideen from which al Qaeda emerged. American and European military intervention in Afghanistan after 2001 has led to failure, chaos, and further radicalization. The invasion of Iraq created ISIS and sparked a regional war. American operations against the "legitimate" regime of Bashar al Assad in Syria fuel both ISIS and al Qaeda there. Indeed, Putin claims the US is directly supporting al Qaeda against Assad. The US helped overthrow Hosni Mubarak in Egypt and then overthrew Qaddafi, spreading the chaos and violence of the Arab Spring and adding fuel to the Islamist fire. And American hostility toward Iran has prevented a natural ally from playing its rightful part in fighting terrorists.[54]

Putin also accuses the US of fomenting and supporting the "color revolutions" that toppled post-Soviet rulers, especially in Ukraine and Georgia.[55] Those revolutions brought corrupt, incompetent American puppets to power in Tbilisi and Kiev, creating crises that Russia was forced to resolve. When Putin did attempt to protect Russian populations victimized by these Western-sponsored criminal governments, the US rallied its European lackeys to impede and then punish him.

Putin finds it hard to see what benefit America gains from all the disaster and chaos it has caused. He thinks it is clear, however, that the US has shown itself unworthy of the role of hegemon and incapable of exercising it properly. The post–Cold War international order is thus collapsing of its own accord. Russia must help it transition to a new and more stable—multipolar—basis.[56]

Restoring Russian preeminence in the former Soviet states is a first step. Demonstrating the fecklessness of NATO is the next. Gaining the support of European parties and then states will both reestablish Russia's dominant position on the continent and cut America's key proxies away. Reestablishing the Soviet Union's former position in the Middle East will prevent the US from pursuing its disastrous unilateral military policies. In the end the US will have to accept that it is only one of several great powers once more, with a constrained sphere of influence and the obligation to respect Russia's ascendancy in Eastern Europe. That is Putin's aim.[57]

What Do We Do About It All?

Crafting American policy responses to the interwoven strands of Russian revisionisms is difficult. Some parts of that task are easy to articulate, if difficult to execute. Others are hard even to conceive. Any sound strategy for securing the interests of the US and its allies, as well as the survival of international law and any semblance of the current international order, requires cutting through narratives to realities.

Russia has no right to use or threaten the use of force against its neighbors to coerce them to revise the terms of agreements made as the Soviet Union collapsed. The US and NATO have solemn and vital obligations to defend all member states of the alliance against such attacks and threats. Our common strategy must focus on these truths and obligations. We will otherwise allow Putin to rewrite the rules of international affairs to suit the interests of expansionists, revisionists, and dictators around the world.

The Baltic States. The US and NATO must unequivocally and unambiguously defend the Baltic States against Russian threats and provocations. Forward stationing small numbers of forces in those states is a start. Recent

NATO exercises in Eastern Europe were another good signal. Gradual escalation, however, is unlikely to deter Putin. It is more likely to draw him onto an escalation path he might hope to control.

NATO would be wiser to increase the Baltic States' defenses rapidly and dramatically, sending additional ground forces, air defense systems, and coastal defense capabilities. It need not—and probably should not—base advanced attack aircraft in the Baltics in large numbers. Putin likely does not doubt NATO's ability to project air power over its allies, and putting planes at the Russian border is more aggressive than any of the other actions recommended here. Putin will decry them all as acts of aggression and even war, but the West must act on reality rather than his rhetoric.

Western leaders and populations must internalize the reality that deploying Western ground forces and air defense systems to the Baltic States poses no meaningful threat to Russia. NATO has no plans or intent to invade Russia. But what would such an invasion look like, even if it did? It is insane to imagine that a NATO army would drive on Moscow, repeating the experience of Napoleon and the Wehrmacht. NATO armored forces might well encircle St. Petersburg from bases in Estonia, but what then? Turn south and drive on Moscow from a different direction? The notion of a ground invasion of Russia is more absurd than it has been in many decades—and it was always absurd. Deploying NATO ground forces to the Baltic States, therefore, can only ever be defensive.

Stating the requirement for increased deterrent forces in the Baltics and its justification is straightforward. Making it happen in the face of Putin's counterthrusts would be more difficult. But the largest problem will arise from another of Russia's revisionisms—the treatment of ethnic Russians in former Soviet states.

There is no need to rule on the validity of the complaints of those minorities, or of Putin on their behalf, to recognize the problem they pose. Russia has worked to stoke those complaints and these minorities' sense of marginalization for many years, starting under Yeltsin's rule. The leaders of the Baltic States, particularly Latvia, have failed to woo them back or drive them away. The prospect of a manufactured "rebellion" among Russians against the Latvian (or Estonian or even Lithuanian) government is real, and the promised deployment of more NATO troops to the Baltic States could well trigger it.

NATO would then face a conundrum, since the mutual defense clause of the North Atlantic Treaty (Article 5) appears to address external attacks (although it does not say so explicitly).[58] Some NATO members will likely hesitate to confront Russia over what is presented as a domestic insurrection in a member state. NATO was not meant, after all, to provide the tools for its members to maintain domestic order, but rather to defend them against the Soviet Union and its allies. This distinction will be of great moment to a Europe riven by the refugee crisis, Brexit, and other internal concerns.

Success in defending the Baltic States militarily thus rests first and foremost on executing a political strategy to persuade NATO members that an armed insurrection of Russian separatists supported by Moscow must be regarded as an act of aggression by Russia, requiring an Article 5 response. Developing and prosecuting such a strategy should be one of the most urgent undertakings of the Trump administration and of all European leaders who recognize their obligations to their own peoples and the alliance of which they are a part.

Ukraine and Georgia. The situation in Ukraine has already deteriorated far beyond the reach of such defensive measures. Putin has occupied and annexed Crimea and is steadily enhancing its land, sea, and air defenses. His proxies, supported by thousands of Russian troops, control eastern Ukraine and continually press on loyalist forces to their west. The government in Kiev is weak, corrupt, ineffective, and riven by internal rivalries. Populist parties and angry militias threaten its political and physical survival. Russian military forces are being built up all along its frontiers. Putin has managed to establish himself as a mediator in a conflict in which he is also a belligerent, moreover, through the nature of his participation in the Minsk process.[59]

Identifying the military requirements to meet this threat is, once again, relatively straightforward. The Ukrainian loyalist forces require advanced antitank and antiaircraft munitions, which the US and NATO could supply. Such munitions, along with accelerated and expanded training, could allow Kiev to secure its current truncated borders and possibly push back the separatists in the east somewhat. They would not be sufficient to defend Ukraine against a conventional Russian attack, however. Only the credible promise that NATO would come to the defense of Ukraine in the face of such an attack, thereby going to war with Russia, could be relied on to deter Putin.[60]

Any attempt to extract such a credible guarantee from NATO will run afoul of the same problems considered above with the Baltics, only on a much greater scale. In Ukraine's case, however, that political challenge is not the biggest problem. On the contrary, the instability and fragility of the current Ukrainian government gives Putin the real possibility of causing it to collapse, leaving either chaos or a pro-Russian populist movement in its place. NATO will not come to the defense of chaos, and a pro-Russian government will reject and oppose NATO intervention.

The development and execution of a strategy to create a relatively strong government in Kiev that can withstand such pressures is the sine qua non of a serious approach to stopping Putin's depredations where they stand. The US government has focused much of its efforts in Ukraine on this task but, unfortunately, to limited effect. This undertaking must nevertheless be the main priority for US policy in the Trump administration, supplemented by careful efforts to enable Ukrainian forces to defend their current positions through providing advanced defensive weapons and training.

There is little hope of regaining Crimea for Ukraine any time soon. That task would require war or the serious threat of war against Russia. It is hard to imagine how the West could persuade Putin of its willingness to fight another Crimean War other than by starting it, given the weakness of Western policy on Crimea hitherto and the logistical difficulties of preparing for such an undertaking.

The best course for the West is to refuse ever to recognize Russia's annexation of Crimea, no matter how permanent it seems to have become. The US never recognized the Soviet Union's seizure of the Baltic States in 1939, after all. Official government maps throughout the Cold War showed those states as part of the USSR, with an asterisk explaining the refusal to recognize their reconquest. That asterisk no doubt seemed a silly affectation to many. It helped facilitate the alacrity with which the Baltic States regained their independence as the Soviet system collapsed, however. It is a good model for the right approach to Crimea.

The West should adopt a similar approach to Georgia, particularly the areas of South Ossetia and Abkhazia, which Russian forces helped detach from Georgia in 2008 and which Putin then annexed. Defending the independence of the rump Georgian state should be a priority to which NATO should be prepared to devote military and political resources. It is bound up with not only the survival of other former Soviet states but also fundamental principles of international law.

The Larger Problem. Outlining strategies for halting the Russian reconquest of Ukraine and Georgia is relatively easy, although implementing those strategies may well encounter insurmountable obstacles. Dealing with the larger aims of Russian revisionism is a much more complex and daunting task. The most important element of that task has little initially to do with Russia, however.

Putin's international revisionism and his hopes of restoring Russia to a nearly coequal status with the US rest and feed on the West's fear of decline and failure. As long as the West doubts itself or, worse still, believes itself to be the author of the world's woes and its own suffering, confronting Putin's efforts to redraft the global order is hopeless. The US in particular, and its allies as well, must recommit themselves to bearing the burden of global leadership, recognizing that failure and responsibility for mistakes is a core part of that burden. Only then can they contest with Putin for the leadership role.

The challenges posed by the requirements to redefine "Russia" and "Russians" and address the failings of the post-1991 settlements will remain important even after Putin's internationalist revisionism is defeated (assuming it is). Solving those problems is not a lesser task in getting Putin to back down. It is much harder.

It will depend, however, on the resolution of the current crisis in Ukraine. If Putin's efforts to regain control of the Soviet lands lead to war, then the peace ending that war will become the new basis for dealing with these problems. The drafters of that peace would do well to keep that fact in mind. Such a war is both unlikely and undesirable, however, and so the most difficult challenge of all remains how to persuade a people to accept a redefinition of many centuries of identity, much to their detriment, and to adjust peacefully to agreements they increasingly find intolerable.

The answer lies in the nature of the Russian regime itself. Putin has acted on Russia's revisionisms, as he has consolidated power and moved Russia away from the liberal democratic order of the 1990s. The past decade and a half do indeed appear to validate the argument that Aron and others made during the Yeltsin period—that Russia could have freedom or empire but not both. Economic calamity and postrevolutionary disappointment discredited freedom for many Russians. But they are now seeing that they can also be unfree and poor and disappointed as well. The best strategy that the West can pursue toward Russia now is to continue to force Russians to confront that choice.

The West, with the United States at its head, must persuade Putin and the Russian people to accept the terms they themselves negotiated for the post–Cold War settlement—or renegotiate those terms on an equal basis and in peace with their neighbors. We must persuade Russia that it will lose another confrontation and that the consequences of another loss will be even worse than those of 1991. We must cajole Russia into developing a new national identity not bound in the subjugation of a large empire and military might but rather as a peaceful democratic state with an ancient tradition and a future of hope.

We will have to accept conflict and the risk of war to succeed in this task, although we should do everything possible to minimize the one and avoid the other. But the path to enduring peace lies through confrontation, backed by determination and force. There is no other way.

Notes

1. For a detailed discussion of the changing American position on the future relationship between Germany and NATO, including the assurances provided at various points to Mikhail Gorbachev, see George H. W. Bush and Brent Scowcroft, *A World Transformed* (New York: Alfred A Knopf, 1998), chaps. 10 and 11.

2. This essay owes much to the superb work of Leon Aron, particularly *Roads to the Temple*, which demonstrates with marvelous clarity that the collapse of the Soviet Union resulted from a revolution launched unintentionally by Mikhail Gorbachev's policy of glasnost. Leon Aron, *Roads to the Temple: Truth, Memory, Ideas, and Ideals in the Making of the Russian Revolution, 1987–1991* (New Haven, CT: Yale University Press, 2012).

3. The issue of citizenship for Russian speakers in the Baltic States was one of the most contentious and has been the basis for Russian efforts against Baltic governments ever since. Latvian and Estonian refusals to grant citizenship or passports to those who had immigrated to their countries during the Soviet occupation seemed to Moscow a betrayal of promises to provide fairly for Russians "stranded," as Putin would have it, in suddenly independent former Soviet republics. For a detailed discussion of this issue (albeit from a perspective highly critical of Moscow), see Agnia Grigas, *Beyond Crimea: The New Russian Empire* (New Haven, CT: Yale University Press, 2016), chap. 5.

4. Putin's address to Russia's Federation Council on the "reunification" of Crimea with Russia offers one of the clearest statements of this view. Vladimir Putin, "Address by President of the Russian Federation" (speech, Moscow, March 18, 2014), http://en.kremlin.ru/events/president/news/20603.

5. President George H. W. Bush made clear his determination to follow the Soviet recognition of Baltic independence rather than leading it: "But we were striving for a permanent resolution of the issue. That could best be achieved only through voluntary Soviet recognition of Baltic independence. Otherwise, should the nationalist right ever come to power, they could more easily reverse the situation, claiming the USSR acted only under duress in a weakened condition. In other words, they could allege that the independence was not valid. By being patient for a few days until Moscow acted on its own volition, we prevented the possibility of anyone successfully asserting this claim." Bush and Scowcroft, *A World Transformed.*

6. Aron, *Roads to the Temple*, 25.

7. For a concise discussion of the origins and early developments of nationalist movements in Ukraine and Belarus, see Richard Pipes, *The Formation of the Soviet Union* (Cambridge, MA: Harvard University Press, 1954), 7–12.

8. See the various excellent works of Edward A. Allworth and Martha Brill Olcott, as well as Pipes, *The Formation of the Soviet Union.*

9. The defection of Ukraine was particularly shocking, even to Yeltsin. Aron, *Roads to the Temple*, 475.

10. Vladimir Putin, "Annual Address to the Federal Assembly of the Russian Federation" (speech, Moscow, April 25, 2005), http://en.kremlin.ru/events/president/transcripts/22931.

11. See Putin, "Address by President of the Russian Federation."

12. Perhaps the most important and controversial document was the Agreement for

the Formation of the Commonwealth of Independent States, signed on December 12, 1991, by the leaders of the Russian Federation, the Belarussian Republic, and Ukraine. Aron, *Roads to the Temple*, 477. The document is available at https://rg.ru/1991/12/19/sng-site-dok.html.

13. Grigas, *Beyond Crimea*, 152–53.

14. Pipes, *The Formation of the Soviet Union*. This statement is likely to offend nationalists in these countries, who fiercely defend the unique nationhood of their peoples and may regard any questioning of it as a threat to the integrity of their states. It is important to separate these two issues. The peoples of Ukraine, Belarus, and the other former republics have full rights to their independent states that are not dependent on proving anything about the history of their nationalisms. One can and should recognize the obligation to defend them as constituent members of the community of states without accepting nationalist narratives that exaggerate their distinctness from their neighbors—as nationalist narratives almost always do.

15. Grigas discusses the evolution of the term "conationalists" at length in *Beyond Crimea*. Grigas, *Beyond Crimea*, chap. 3.

16. For a list of pre-Putin-era documents relating to this issue, see Grigas, *Beyond Crimea*, table 1, 67–68.

17. William E. Odom, *The Collapse of the Soviet Military* (New Haven, CT: Yale University Press, 2000), 297–301.

18. Ukraine's agreement to hand over the nuclear weapons on its territory to Russia was cemented by the Budapest Memorandums on Security Assurances of December 5, 1994. See Council on Foreign Relations, "Budapest Memorandums on Security Assurances," December 5, 1994, accessed September 28, 2016, http://www.cfr.org/nonproliferation-arms-control-and-disarmament/budapest-memorandums-security-assurances-1994/p32484. The agreement committed Russia, the UK, and the US "to respect the independence and sovereignty and the existing borders of Ukraine."

19. Leon Aron, *Yeltsin: A Revolutionary Life* (New York: St. Martin's Press, 2000), 668–69.

20. The formal treaty governing the division of the Black Sea Fleet was signed on May 28, 1997. Soglashenie mezhdu Rossisskoi Federatsiei i Ukrainioi o Statuse i Usloviiakh Prebyvaniia Chernomorskogo Flota Rossiiskoi Federatsii na Territorii Ukrainy, May 28, 1997.

21. Putin, "Address by President of the Russian Federation."

22. The Russian Duma approved a proposal by Putin to renounce this treaty unilaterally on March 31, 2014. See TASS, "State Duma Approves Denunciation of Russian-Ukrainian Agreements on Black Sea Fleet," March 31, 2014, http://tass.com/Russia/725964. Official documents posted on the Kremlin website offer no explanation or justification for the renunciation of Russia's international obligations.

23. Again, it is vital not to be deceived by superficial similarities. German nationalists and Hitler claimed that "historically" German territories, such as the corridor separating the enclave of Danzig (now Gdansk) from Germany or the Sudetenland area of the new Czechoslovak state, had been unjustly stripped from postwar Germany. These arguments seem parallel with Putin's complaints about Crimea, Eastern Ukraine, and other such territories. But the Weimar and Hitlerite complaint was against a treaty imposed on

Germany by victorious powers after a military defeat, whereas Russia never suffered such a defeat and entered voluntarily into the agreements that gave away parts of its territory. The distinction is important. Hitler could claim that he was simply righting a historical wrong done to Germany by outside powers. Putin can argue only that he is unilaterally renegotiating the terms of deals Yeltsin should not have made.

24. Aron, *Yeltsin.* Yeltsin himself recognized and lamented the limitations of his accomplishments in the odd speech he delivered on New Year's Eve 1999, in which he announced his resignation and the transfer of power to Putin. "I want to ask your forgiveness," he said to his people, "for the fact that many of our common dreams did not become reality. And what seemed easy to us turned out to be tortuously difficult. I ask forgiveness for the fact that I did not justify some of the hopes of those people who believed that we could in one tug, one stroke leap from the gray, stagnant, totalitarian past into a bright, rich, civilized future. I myself believed that we could. It seemed that it needed only one tug and we would overcome all. But we did not have one tug. To some extent I was too naïve. Some of the problems turned out to be too difficult. We waded forward through mistakes, through failures. Many people experienced upheavals in this difficult time. But I want you to know." Boris Yeltsin, "I Have Taken a Decision. I Am Leaving. Farewell Address of Boris N. Yeltsin" (speech, December 31, 1999).

25. For a superb and detailed narrative of Stalin's calculations and miscalculations in this period, see Gabriel Gorodetsky, *Grand Delusion: Stalin and the German Invasion of Russia* (New Haven, CT: Yale University Press, 2001).

26. This section draws heavily on Leon Aron, "Who Are We?" in *Roads to the Temple: Truth, Memory, Ideas, and Ideals in the Making of the Russian Revolution, 1987–1991* (New Haven, CT: Yale University Press, 2012).

27. Vicki L. Hesli and William M. Reisinger, *The 1999–2000 Elections in Russia: Their Impact and Legacy* (New York: Cambridge University Press, 2011), chap. 1; and Aron, *Yeltsin.*

28. Dmitrii Medvedev reportedly said in 2012 that Yeltsin had stolen the 1996 election, fueling claims that Yeltsin's victory was fraudulent. See, for example, Simon Shuster, "Rewriting Russian History: Did Boris Yeltsin Steal the 1996 Presidential Election?," *Time,* February 24, 2012, http://content.time.com/time/world/article/0,8599,2107565,00.html.

29. Putin won by more than 20 percentage points, capturing 52.57 percent of the vote. See Michael Wines, "Election in Russia: The Overview; Putin Wins Russia Vote in First Round, but His Majority Is Less Than Expected," *New York Times,* March 27, 2000, http://www.nytimes.com/2000/03/27/world/election-russia-overview-putin-wins-russia-vote-first-round-but-his-majority.html.

30. Aron, *Yeltsin,* chap. 13.

31. Vladimir Putin, "Open Letter to Voters," February 25, 2000, http://en.kremlin.ru/events/president/transcripts/24144.

32. C. T. Evans, trans., "Russian Primary Chronicle (Excerpts)," http://novaonline.nvcc.edu/eli/evans/his101/documents/chronicle.html.

33. Putin's speeches are filled with references to Russia's "thousand-year" history and culture: "In order to revive national consciousness, we need to link historical eras and get back to understanding the simple truth that Russia did not begin in 1917 or even in 1991, but rather, that we have a common, continuous history spanning over one thousand

years, and we must rely on it to find inner strength and purpose in our national development." Vladimir Putin, "Address to the Federal Assembly" (speech, Moscow, December 12, 2012), http://en.kremlin.ru/events/president/news/17118.

34. Putin, "Address by President of the Russian Federation."

35. A. S. Pushkin, "The Bronze Horseman," 1837, stanza 3, lines 6–7.

36. Putin, "Annual Address to the Federal Assembly of the Russian Federation." This statement deftly addresses two perennial arguments in Russian ideology and history. Slavophiles, such as Leo Tolstoy and other less gifted 19th-century writers, argue that Russia has always been distinct from Europe and must avoid borrowing too deeply from European traditions. Westernizers, of which Peter the Great was the first and most important, argue that Russia is rightfully a European power. However, the Westernizers generally faced the problem that Western Europe has historically regarded Russia as backward and Asiatic—hence Putin's simultaneous declaration of Russia's Europeanness and claim that Russia was never more backward than any other European state. But Putin will also embrace parts of the Slavophile argument in defense of Russia's uniqueness, as we shall see below.

37. Putin, "Annual Address to the Federal Assembly of the Russian Federation."

38. Putin has steadily expanded the list of Russian Navy ships named for these heroes. See Frederick W. Kagan, "What's in a Name? Putin's Ominous Vision for Russia," Fox News, July 13, 2016, http://www.foxnews.com/opinion/2016/07/13/whats-in-name-putins-ominous-vision-for-russia.html.

39. "The Russias" include Great Russia, the heartland of the Russian Federation; "White Russia," or Belarus; and "Little Russia," or Ukraine. The Romanovs styled themselves emperors of all the Russias, **императоры всероссийские**, and the word "all-Russian," or **всероссийский**, remains in use as a synonym for "Russian" with an archaic flavor. Russians are not really distinguishable from the lands they inhabit, which are rightfully Russian lands in this traditional view.

40. Putin, "Address by President of the Russian Federation."

41. Aron, *Roads to the Temple.*

42. It is impossible to overstate the degree to which the current Russian state narrative rests on identifying Russia as "free" and "democratic." Yeltsin established that narrative in the 1990s as the predominant achievement of his reign and of Russia's painful post–Cold War tribulations. Putin often modifies it by noting that Russia's history of representative government is distinctive and should not blindly follow Western models. But he would have to develop an entirely new identity and ideology for the current regime were he openly to abandon democratic and representative principles. A sample from his 2012 Address to the Federal Assembly is typical: "Democracy is the only political choice for Russia. I would like to stress that we share the universal democratic principles adopted worldwide. However, Russia's democracy means the power of the Russian people with their own traditions of self-rule and not the fulfillment of standards imposed on us from the outside." Vladimir Putin, "Address to the Federal Assembly" (speech, Moscow, December 12, 2012), http://en.kremlin.ru/events/president/news/17118.

43. Henry Meyer, Ilya Arkhipov, and Stepan Kravchenko, "Putin's Party Gains Crushing Win in Parliamentary Elections," Bloomberg, September 18, 2016, https://www.bloomberg.com/news/articles/2016-09-18/putin-s-united-russia-gets-45-in-duma-election-exit-poll-shows.

44. This narrative is obvious from the exaggerations Putin regularly makes about the Western military threat to Russia. For example, he has falsely accused NATO of ignoring its obligations under the Conventional Forces in Europe Treaty. He described the planned deployment of a highly limited antiballistic missile system in Europe that could not shoot down Russian missiles aimed at the US, but could only interdict Iranian missiles aimed at Europe, as "elements of US strategic weapons systems." Vladimir Putin, "Annual Address to the Federal Assembly" (speech, Moscow, April 26, 2007). Nor is Putin the only Russian leader to do so. Dmitrii Medvedev used his first address as president in 2008 to say, "I would add something about what we have had to face in recent years . . . the construction of a global missile defence system, the installation of military bases around Russia, the unbridled expansion of NATO and other similar 'presents' for Russia—we therefore have every reason to believe that they are simply testing our strength." Dmitrii Medvedev, "Address to the Federal Assembly of the Russian Federation" (speech, November 5, 2008).

45. Vladimir Putin et al., *First Person: An Astonishingly Frank Self-Portrait by Russia's President Vladimir Putin*, trans. Catherine A. Fitzpatrick (New York: Public Affairs, 2000).

46. Kathleen Weinberger, "Putin's Gambit in Ukraine: Strategic Implications," Institute for the Study of War, September 3, 2016, http://iswresearch.blogspot.com/2016/09/putins-gambit-in-ukraine-strategic.html. Putin may have attempted to influence the US presidential election in favor of Donald Trump, who has taken a strong pro-Putin stance, but this paper will not explore that controversy.

47. Leon Aron, "Drivers of Putin's Foreign Policy," testimony before the Committee on Foreign Affairs, US House of Representatives, June 14, 2016, https://www.aei.org/publication/drivers-of-putins-foreign-policy/.

48. President Bill Clinton referred to the US as an indispensable nation. Sid Blumenthal, Clinton's adviser, is said to have coined the phrase. See James Mann, "On Realism, Old and New," *American Prospect*, October 29, 2014, http://prospect.org/article/realism-old-and-new-0.

49. The issue of promises made to Russia regarding NATO's expansion is complex. A NATO document addresses them in a relatively balanced fashion: Michael Rühle, "NATO Enlargement and Russia: Myths and Realities," http://www.nato.int/docu/review/2014/Russia-Ukraine-Nato-crisis/Nato-enlargement-Russia/EN/index.htm. Bush and Scowcroft discuss their negotiations over the reunification of Germany in detail. See Bush and Scowcroft, *A World Transformed*, chap. 10. The NATO-Russia Founding Act states that NATO members do not intend to deploy nuclear forces on the territory of new member states and suggests (but does not promise) that NATO will seek to avoid stationing significant additional conventional forces as well. Founding Act on Mutual Relations, Cooperation and Security Between NATO and the Russian Federation, NATO-Russ., May 27, 1997, https://www.nato.int/cps/en/natohq/official_texts_25468.htm.

50. For Putin's use of the Kosovo precedent, see Putin, "Address by President of the Russian Federation."

51. Jill Dougherty, "Putin Warns on Iraq War," CNN, March 28, 2003, http://www.cnn.com/2003/WORLD/europe/03/28/sprj.irq.putin/.

52. Ellen Barry, "Putin Criticizes West for Libya Incursion," *New York Times*, April 26, 2011, http://www.nytimes.com/2011/04/27/world/europe/27putin.html.

53. Tom Parfitt, "Vladimir Putin Vows That United States 'Will Never Subjugate Russia,'" *Telegraph*, November 8, 2014, http://www.telegraph.co.uk/news/worldnews/vladimir-putin/11239052/Vladimir-Putin-vows-that-United-States-will-never-subjugate-Russia.html.

54. Putin has outlined these complaints most aggressively at two speeches to the Valdai Club, one in 2014 and one in 2016. Vladimir Putin, "Meeting of the Valdai International Discussion Club" (speech, Sochi, October 24, 2014), http://en.kremlin.ru/events/president/news/46860; and Vladmir Putin, "Meeting of the Valdai International Discussion Club" (speech, Sochi, October 27, 2016), http://en.kremlin.ru/events/president/news/53151.

55. Dennis Lynch, "Russian Security Council Warns US Seeks 'Color Revolution' Against Kremlin," *International Business Times*, March 25, 2016, http://www.ibtimes.com/russian-security-council-warns-us-seeks-color-revolution-against-kremlin-1859808.

56. Paul R. Gregory, "Putin's New World Order," *Politico*, September 29, 2015, http://www.politico.eu/article/putin-new-world-order-syria-united-nations-new-york/.

57. Kathleen Weinberger, "Putin Sets the Stage for the Incoming U.S. Administration," Institute for the Study of War, November 30, 2016, http://www.understandingwar.org/backgrounder/putin-sets-stage-incoming-us-administration.

58. The North Atlantic Treaty, April 4, 1949, http://www.nato.int/cps/en/natohq/official_texts_17120.htm.

59. Hugo Spaulding, "Putin's Next Objectives in the Ukraine Crisis," Institute for the Study of War, February 3, 2015, http://www.understandingwar.org/sites/default/files/Ukraine%20backgrounder_V6.pdf.

60. Franklin Holcomb, *The Order of Battle of the Ukrainian Armed Forces: A Key Component in European Security*, Institute for the Study of War, December 9, 2016, http://www.understandingwar.org/sites/default/files/ISW%20Ukrainian%20ORBAT%20Holcomb%202016_0.pdf.

2

China:
The Imperial Legacy

DAN BLUMENTHAL

It is now evident that the People's Republic of China (PRC) seeks to revise the balance of power in East Asia and eventually become the region's hegemon. Over the past decade Beijing has accelerated its military modernization program, aggressively pressed its maritime claims in the South and East China Seas, coerced and isolated Taiwan, and continued to challenge the United States for control of what is known as "the first island chain": countries and islets from Japan to parts of Indonesia that to China appear as a potentially linked fence locking it out of the Pacific and Indian Oceans.

This chapter will explore four features of the PRC's revisionism. First, China's rise is actually a resurgence to power or, as Party General Secretary Xi Jinping has put it, a "national rejuvenation."[1] The country has a long imperial history as the central power in Asia. China sees itself as *returning* to its once-dominant imperial preeminence. Given China's thousands of years of history, Chinese leaders view their loss of power and influence less than 200 years ago as an aberration from the natural order of things—an order with China at its center.

Second, China seeks a new order based on this imperial Sinosphere, both in its physical boundaries and its worldview. In a sense, that order already exists. Beijing rules over the world's last remaining multiethnic empire, having reacquired most of its territories after the Qing dynasty's collapse. While the Ottoman and various European empires were divided into separate nation-states that we now know as Europe, the Middle East, and Central Asia, this was never fully the case with China. However, its ambitions do not end there. Beijing views maritime East Asia partly through imperial lenses, claiming historic rights to Taiwan and what others view as international waters or their own sovereign territory.

Third, though China must often behave in accord with the norms and historic patterns of a "normal" nation-state, its dominant personality is that of an empire. With more power and prestige, it seeks to reorder the Asian political order to its liking. This means that China not only wants to do what any rising power would do—create more strategic depth, gain more influence in its surrounding seas, and dilute the influence of the extant hegemon—but also believes that the territories it claims and the countries that contest them should be deferential to the Middle Kingdom and should not be regarded as equals.

Fourth, there are constraints on China's global ambitions, in particular its embrace of the global economic order. For the time being, it accepts US management of the international financial system and the global US military presence that keeps the world safe for maritime trade. While Beijing has become more active in the Middle East (including constructing a naval base in Djibouti), its major territorial ambitions and bid for power primacy are presently limited to the Asia-Pacific. China could challenge the global order more directly if, for example, it found that order threatening to the continued primacy of the Chinese Communist Party (CCP).[2] For now, China lives uncomfortably within that order, garnering its benefits and using them to build up its instruments of power while also guarding against the most intrusive elements. While the focus of China's revisionism is Asia, if it succeeds in rejuvenating itself to Asia predominance, it will inevitably become a global competitor to the United States.

Resurgence to Power

The political challenge for all Chinese leaders since the fall of the Qing dynasty has been that China is an empire operating inside a world order meant for nation-states. Or, as Lucian Pye wrote in 1990, China is still more of a "civilization pretending to be a nation state."[3] Since the Western powers began to challenge the Qing Empire in the late 18th century, China's most basic strategic need has been to "make the world safe" for the Chinese empire.

Many aspects of China's core political, social, and cultural mores, developed over thousands of years of Chinese history, still shape its geostrategic actions. These include the quasi-religious beliefs that Chinese rulers have a Mandate of Heaven to rule "all under heaven"; that Chinese civilization is superior, more virtuous, and more benign than that of the West; that hierarchy leads to order; and that sometimes the state needs to use great violence to quell uprisings, drive back invaders, and gain the compliance of tributaries.[4] In particular, Chinese elites have learned that the greatest threat to Chinese dynasties has been when internal uprising and external pressure have coincided. When "harmony" is threatened, such as a country in the Sinosphere not acting with due deference to Beijing, violence can be used to restore it.

The CCP's ideological foundation was revolutionary Leninism, and therefore Mao sought to purge China of the vestiges of what he derided as the weakness of the old Confucian political order. Even so, Mao ruled a multiethnic empire that had similar borders to those of the Qing and expected deference from the Asian periphery. The idea of Middle Kingdom centrality would not be purged from China's strategic DNA.

Further, the CCP today derives its legitimacy in part from its economic performance and in part from its claim to reverse the "century of humiliation," which, in China's view, is a historical aberration that needs to be avenged as China restores itself to its rightful place of greatness.[5] Party Secretary Xi Jinping's "China Dream" doctrine has made the latter more explicit: He promises to rejuvenate China.[6] Moreover, the CCP now openly celebrates China's imperial past. Xi announced his new national plans at the national museum that now proudly exhibits China's imperial history:

> The "revival" narrated in the museum exhibit is also built on a new kind of memory of China's imperial past (from roughly 221 BCE to 1911). In the Mao era, China's long dynastic history was usually denigrated as a time when the Chinese people suffered under the yoke of feudalism and the aristocratic, land-owning class—in league with the ruling imperial houses—oppressed the peasants. Today, this Maoist view of the imperial past has been replaced with a much more positive and lustrous image that reflects China's new global, "imperial" aspirations in the present . . . what is being "revived" in China today is the greatness and ancient glory of China's past lost to Western and Japanese imperialism. The

restoration of Confucianism . . . both in Party and popular dis-
course, parallels this revisionist view of the imperial past.[7]

What Is the Imperial Past? The Height of Chinese Power

To understand what the CCP is attempting to reclaim, one must understand
China at the height of its power. Modern China's boundaries are loosely based
on those established at the peak of the Qing dynasty, which ruled from 1636
until 1911. The Qing dynasty was founded by the Manchus, a nomadic tribal
people from the Asiatic steppe, who toppled the Ming dynasty (1368–1644),
reconquered lost Ming lands, and expanded the Chinese empire.

To expand outward from the Han heartland, successive emperors
mounted military campaigns. Kangxi, the first great Manchu/Qing emperor,
pushed the empire north, establishing new borders with Russia, fighting the
Mongols, and stationing troops in Tibet.

China had the unique ability to "Sinify" both peripheral territories and
its own invaders, such as the Manchus. The Manchu ruling elite maintained
a distinct identity from the Han Chinese, but they also adopted important
dimensions of traditional Chinese political culture. They did this in part
to pacify the majority Han population and in part because the Confucian
political-social structure seemed an efficient means to rule an empire.

After their initial conquest of China, the Qing emperors possessed a large
battle-hardened military but worried that these very troops would cause
unrest or start a civil war.[8] Thus, the Qing emperors turned to the traditional "Chinese" Confucian-based examination and civil-service system to
gain social and political control.

In foreign affairs, as with past Chinese dynasties, the Manchus used a host
of military and diplomatic means to conquer, govern, and defend the empire
and its domain. Beijing reestablished a tributary model of relations within a
core Sinic zone—Korea, Siam (Thailand), Vietnam, Burma, and the Ryukyu
Islands. These states were Sinic in that elites often spoke Chinese, adulated
Chinese culture, and accepted the ethics and norms of a Confucian state.
The elites and much of the population practiced the same quasi-religious
rituals and internalized many of the same Confucian and Buddhist beliefs
of the Han. Tributary emissaries interacted with the Chinese court through

a set of elaborate rituals, including the kowtow, meant to acknowledge Chinese supremacy.

What is now known as maritime East Asia was thus Sino-centric. Here is how the historian John Fairbank puts it:

> The Chinese tended to think of their foreign relations as giving expression externally to the same principles of social and political order that was manifested internally. . . . China's foreign relations were accordingly hierarchic and non-egalitarian.[9]

As long as his rule was consistent with Confucian notions of virtue, the Chinese emperor was the universal ruler of "all under heaven." This way of thinking left no room for a plurality of sovereigns in international relations, let alone the new European concept of sovereign equality among nations. Chinese leaders believed that as long as they ruled "virtuously," they had the legitimacy to treat other nations as a Chinese father would a son.

"Sinicization" was an important tool of statecraft, but shared cultural ties alone did not preserve the tributary system. Instead, vassal states were cowed by Chinese power as well. The Qing dynasty twice invaded Korea to remove leaders who continued to support the Ming dynasty's claim to be the true rulers in Beijing. When the Koreans finally bowed to the Qing, it was largely out of fear of Chinese military might rather than respect for Chinese cultural norms.

Outside the Sinic zone, the Manchus marched west, seeking to create a multiethnic empire comprised of Mongols, Tibetans, Turkic peoples, Han Chinese, and dozens of smaller tribes that accepted the precepts of Chinese civilization. To expand from the Han heartland—modern China's eastern seaboard—successive Qing emperors mounted campaigns of conquest.

The Qing relied on their strict banner system of military organization to expand the empire's western reaches. The banners were military units akin to Roman legions. During wartime, each banner acted as a self-contained military force. Moreover, the banners' bureaucratic structure allowed the emperor to pay salaries, distribute land, and administer justice to his troops. Conquered forces, such as the Mongols, were incorporated into the Chinese imperial army, organized into their own banner units, and commanded by Manchu officers.

Under the reign of Emperor Kangxi (1661–1722), Qing banner men brought the Chinese empire to the height of its power and prestige. At the beginning of his rule, Kangxi consolidated power, putting down rival feudal lords in southern China. With the center of the empire unified, he turned to invade Taiwan, seizing it from a former and recalcitrant Ming military leader, Gen. Zheng Chenggong. Next, the emperor pushed the empire northward and westward, establishing a border with Russia, campaigning against the Mongols, and stationing troops in Tibet.

Qing foreign policy in Central Asia did not fit neatly into the tributary system. Instead, Qing statecraft turned to what moderns would call realpolitik—conquest, diplomacy, and alliances with local elites based on power, as well as acceptance and pandering to Central Asian cultural norms. The historian Peter Perdue writes:

> Tributary views were only one of a variety of Chinese world views. . . . Before the 1750s (when the continental threat had been exterminated), Qing elites knew, quite well, that they were engaged in a long-term military struggle with rival Central Eurasian states which had equal claims to legitimacy. The Kangxi emperor, in appealing for Mongolian support, most frequently invoked the common heritage of the Manchus and Mongols as Central Eurasians, or he appealed to Buddhist conceptions of universal benevolence, rather than Confucian hierarchy. He knew that these appeals were more convincing than invoking his stature as the Son of Heaven.[10]

Although they could adapt their diplomacy to the diverse political cultures they sought to dominate, Kangxi and his grandson Qianlong could be extremely violent. For example, the Mongols eventually were crushed. In the 1750s, Qianlong imposed his final solution, killing Mongol Zunghar elites and incorporating their territories into one region, which he called Xinjiang—a new Chinese frontier. Under Qianlong, China was at the height of its power. As historian Odd Arne Westad writes:

> By the 1750s it [China] had crushed the political and military independence of all the smaller nations on its northern frontier

and begun incorporating them into a much-enlarged China. It had regulated its relations with its remaining neighbors, from the Russian empire in the north to the kingdoms in Southeast Asia and in the Himalayas, according to Chinese preconditions and based on a Chinese sense of superiority. By the middle part of the eighteenth century, the Qing empire had created a world in eastern Asia that was almost entirely its own.[11]

Indeed, the Qianlong emperor was renowned for his Ten Great Campaigns to exert control and subdue dissent in Burma, Mongolia, Sichuan China, Taiwan, Tibet, Vietnam, and Xinjiang.[12] He was willing to pay great costs and take great risks on behalf of expansion. For example, the Chinese lost 70,000 soldiers in an unsuccessful campaign in Burma. A similar outcome occurred in Vietnam in the late 1780s, when the Qing lost thousands of soldiers in an attempt to intervene in the Vietnamese civil war on behalf of their favored rulers.

While imperial statecraft imposed a softer tributary system on the Sinic core, getting foreign elites to accept Beijing's superiority sometimes required massive violence. Qing statecraft was successful until the West turned its gaze to China.

Imperial Downfall

The empire's worldview, however, carried the roots of its own destruction. The Chinese empire refused to accept any country as a sovereign equal. This was problematic particularly because the West was undergoing a revolution in international relations, wherein the principle of state equality was a pillar of a new European system. For this system to work, the West needed a modern diplomatic core that could conduct new relations among nations, professional militaries, and other institutions and instruments that we long ago have come to accept as the pillars of statehood.

In contrast, Chinese rulers saw no need for a modern diplomatic corps or ministry of foreign affairs. Instead, separate ministries were assigned to manage different types of "barbarians." For example, the Office of Border Affairs managed relations with the Mongols, Zunghars, and Russians—the areas from which so many invaders had entered China.[13] The Imperial Household dealt with European missionaries, while the Ministry of Rituals dealt with the neighboring vassal states of Korea, Burma, Thailand, Vietnam, and the Ryukyu Islands. The latter arrangement meant that, with a few important exceptions such as relations with Russia, China saw its most intensive contact with foreigners as a set of rituals that had to be managed.

Chinese concepts of world order were useless against changing global geopolitics, increasingly defined by a quickly industrializing West. Britain was the first to challenge the Qing world order, and Qing mismanagement catalyzed the loss of its sovereignty and much of its territory. In 1784, British Prime Minister William Pitt dispatched the diplomat Lord George Macartney to secure free trade with a restrictive China. It had been over a century since the Qing had negotiated as an equal (with Russia), and unlike his grandfather, the emperor Qianlong did not possess the skill to do so.

Qianlong had no conceptual framework to guide diplomacy with King George. The Qing required of his emissaries the same kowtowing rituals they would have expected from any other mission. The Qing rules and customs required treating the mission as that of another "submissive nation that came bearing tribute and request[ed] benefits from the emperor in return."[14] The Qing seemed to know little about how quickly Britain had industrialized and how powerful it had become.

Macartney would not kowtow. He came as an equal and offered to treat the emperor with the same respect as he would his own king by kneeling before him on one knee. In turn, Qianlong refused all of Macartney's substantive requests. The British would get no permanent embassy and no trade agreement. For the emperor, England was another arrogant barbarian.

Expressing the cultural arrogance and geopolitical ignorance of the Qing world order, Qianlong speculated that perhaps the British had come, like so many Chinese neighbors, to learn Chinese superior ways: "You could not possibly transplant our manners and customs to your alien soil," he wrote the king. He sympathized with the "lonely remoteness" of the British Isles as compared to Beijing, "the hub and center about which all quarters of the globe revolve."[15] For an emperor who had succeeded in consolidating and even expanding beyond the reach of his conquering grandfather, the lack of knowledge about the West was stunning and ultimately disastrous.

The British concluded that the Qing dynasty was not only arrogant and remote but also weak and that it did not understand Western power. The British returned after the Napoleonic wars and eventually fought the Opium Wars, which secured for London ports of trade and extraterritorial legal rights. It inspired the rest of the European colonialists to demand the same from China, and the century of humiliation began.

Qing statecraft was useless against this new challenge. Beijing could not Sinify the British or the rest of Europe, nor did it have the professional military to fight them. These industrialized nations were different from the conquered Qing lands to the west or the Sinosphere to the south and east. Finally, since the Qing did not see the British as sovereign equals, they would not negotiate nor compromise to find common ground.

The Qing's inability to defend itself against the rapacious colonialists and the concurrent rise of anti-Qing/Manchu internal rebellions sent China into a downward spiral of foreign humiliation and internal dissent. These internal challenges sapped the resources the Qing so badly needed for external defense. This helps explain why contemporary China ruthlessly puts down any form of internal dissent today.

These periods, both when the Qing was at the height of their power and when the empire began to collapse under the weight of outside pressure, still significantly influence the CCP. Indeed, the emotional driver of contemporary Chinese foreign policy is the need to assuage China's great humiliation, recapture lost territories, and avenge the treachery of Japan, an Asian country that had never accepted Chinese superiority and had used its great power to crush China.[16]

The Project of Resurgence Begins

In the early 20th century, the collapse of empires was common. The new "republican" government of China would not accept that fate. China's case was unique in that the successor state to the Qing Empire, the Republic of China, succeeded in regaining the Qing Empire's lost territories. While China holds onto a narrative of past weakness and humiliation, in fact, the diplomacy of a war-torn, divided China was a remarkable success. It overturned the new order imposed on it by the Japanese and European colonialists and patched up the empire. As the historian William Kirby writes:

> Da Qing Guo, the vast Qing empire, the multinational and multi-cultural expanse that included Manchuria, Mongolia, Eastern Turkestan and Tibet, among other areas. No Chinese empire had ever been so big for so long as the Qing realm of the Manchus. But the amazing fact of the Republican era is that this space was not only redefined, as "Chinese" and as the sacred soil of China, but also defended diplomatically to such a degree that the borders of the PRC today are essentially those of the Qing, minus only Outer Mongolia. The Qing fell but the empire remained. More accurately, the empire became the basis of the Chinese national state.[17]

No country has this postimperial diplomatic history. The new republican leaders of China simply relabeled the empire, calling it a nation-state, even as it set about governing the same territories. Uniquely, Chinese revisionism began soon after its old order fell; reconstructing the empire has been the primary aim of Chinese statesmen since the Qing's fall in 1911.

Today, a revisionist China also wants to more deeply uproot the status quo: China wants continued international recognition that the boundaries and territories of One China are essentially the same as those of the Qing dynasty at its height, except for Outer Mongolia. The Chinese today have convinced the world that China's unity is somehow the natural order of things, rather than the result of a series of bloody conquests by the Qing regime. Today, Westerners fail to even challenge the premise that China is *owed* the "unity" it established through conquest and repression.

In the wake of the empire, the Republic of China's diplomats also secured a substantial place for China in the new world order made up not of empires, but of nation-states. A weak and divided China was still treated as an important country. It became one of five permanent members of the UN Security Council, received a seat at the table at the Yalta Conference during World War II, and was a wartime ally of the Americans and British. By the end of two world wars, the Chinese had managed to both become part of a new American-led liberal order based on nation-states and emerge as the only country with its imperial borders more or less intact, securing promises from the great powers that the Qing territories would revert to the new Chinese regime.

The tension between the nation of China and its traditional civilizational imperium was evident even in Mao Zedong's revolutionary extremism. The Great Helmsman had little interest in joining the American-led order and had no use for an open trading and financial system or a set of alliances. Furthermore, Mao found some of the order's "norms" to be objectionable and threatening, such as the commitment to human rights in the UN charter.

While Mao committed himself to Marxist-Leninist revolution, many essential foundations of Chinese strategic culture remained. Ultimately, Mao offered a new approach to Sino-centrism. Even as he railed against the "reactionary" old Chinese system, Mao wanted to restore China to primacy in the Asian system. The pathway to Sino-centrism would be leadership through a revolutionary communist foreign policy that sought to overturn American dominance. He provided aid and training to Ho Chi Minh in a communist revolutionary war, trying to turn him into a proto-Maoist, just as Chinese emperors had tried to shape a Confucian elite in the tributaries. Mao also fought to keep the United States from unifying Korea. He supported communist rebel groups in Burma, Thailand, the Philippines, and Malaysia, believing that his form of communism was purer than that of the Soviets.[18]

Ultimately, his Sinicized communism did not succeed. Mao exhausted his country through endless revolutionary projects such as the Great Leap Forward and the Cultural Revolution and by challenging both Cold War superpowers. The rise of a Soviet-Vietnamese alliance and the increasing hostility between Moscow and Beijing left China isolated and under threat. Backed into a strategic corner, Mao became a practitioner of modern statecraft. As the Soviets threatened war, Mao courted the Americans for support.[19] He successfully sought to regain a place as a permanent member of the UN Security Council and set the stage for Deng Xiaoping to lead China firmly into the family of nations.

A "Normal" Revisionist?

In terms of Beijing's conduct of international relations, Deng Xiaoping led China into the family of nations. However, even the relatively more modern and liberal Deng gave no thought to letting go of China's imperial holdings. There was no compromise on Tibet or Xinjiang's independence, Hong Kong's reversion, or the insistence that Taiwan was part of One China.[20] This is even more remarkable given that Deng's rule coincided with the dissolution of the Soviet empire.

Even as he held onto the imperial territories, Deng did his best to embrace the international system. China took its place at the UN, signed many treaties, joined several multilateral institutions, entered the World Trade Organization, and generally embraced the liberal economic order. China's diplomacy was of a traditional Westphalian character, even taking more seriously the norm of sovereign equality and noninterference in other countries' domestic affairs than the original Westphalian nations. The contradictions and tensions between nation and empire could be put aside for a time.

Accepting the premises of nation-state diplomacy did not mean only peaceful and commercial approaches. Indeed, Deng and his successors never lost sight of the potential efficacy of using force, as Deng launched an ambitious program to strengthen China's science and technology capabilities and engaged in a comprehensive military modernization program. These efforts are in keeping with the long-standing Chinese belief in the efficacy of violence and coercion as tools of statecraft.

It is important to recite the fruits of these military labors, as it is easy to be lulled into a sense that China's approach to hard power is different from the West's because of its Confucian heritage and rhetorical emphasis on harmony. Here are some highlights of that effort.

Since 1990, China has invested in all classes of ballistic and cruise missiles under the world's most active missile program.[21] Its Second Artillery missile force is lethal and now largely precision guided. China has also upgraded its nuclear forces, including road-mobile, solid-fuel intercontinental ballistic missiles capable of striking anywhere in the United States.[22] China similarly developed nuclear submarines that can deploy submarine-launched ballistic missiles. No country has a missile program as active as China's.[23]

According to the Rand Corporation's 2015 US-China military scorecard, the People's Liberation Army (PLA) air forces have also been the beneficiaries of the CCP's largesse: Today, about half (736 of 1,432) of China's fighters are modern, fourth-generation aircraft, the equivalent of American

F-15s, F-16s, and F/A-18s. Yet it is the improvement in PLA maritime forces that has caught the attention of Asia-Pacific leaders. As Rand noted in its report:

> Clearly, the PLA Navy's surface fleet has made remarkable strides. As late as 2003, only about 14 percent of its destroyers and 24 percent of its frigates might have been considered modern—capable of operations against a capable enemy. By 2015, those figures had risen to 65 percent and 69 percent, respectively.[24]

China has been acquiring modern diesel-powered submarines at a faster clip than any other military in the world. It is now fielding modern destroyers at a rapid rate, many of them equipped with capable antiair defenses and long-range, antiship cruise missiles. China has also developed the world's first operational antiship ballistic missile, specifically designed for targeting American aircraft carriers.[25] Furthermore, in a general surprise to most observers, China remains committed to building its own aircraft carriers and mastering carrier aviation.[26]

Crucially, the PLA has also focused on improving its battle networking—the connective military tissue that allows for command-and-control and improved targeting.[27] In combination, these systems expand the Chinese capability to hit targets further into the first island chain, or the string of nearby American-allied countries that includes Japan, Taiwan, and the Philippines. All this adds up to a break in the US monopoly over what Russia calls the "precision strike regime"—the network of communications and information systems that tie together the navy, air force, and missile force capability to find, target, and destroy American and allied forces and military installations. The PLA can now project power throughout the South and East China Seas and increasingly into the Indian Ocean.

The clearest sign of Chinese revisionism is that China's military modernization has changed the balance of power in the Asia-Pacific. This is all a far cry from the Qing banner system of military organization and Mao's revolutionary forces. In a consequential turn of history since the British-visited destruction of China, it is Beijing that has invested more time, energy, and resources into building a modern force that could do unto others what was once done to China.

At the same time, China improved its capacity for imperial defense against a restive populace and periphery. In many ways, China is the most sophisticated police state in the world.[28]

The military buildup and increased uses of coercive power are consistent with China's revisionism. Much of that power is aimed at Taiwan, as China tries to get the democratic island to "rejoin" the motherland. The obsessive focus on "regaining" Taiwan is consistent with imperial thinking—"all under heaven," or at least all of what the Qing once ruled, must again be ruled by Beijing.

However, alongside this conception is the thinking of the new Chinese maritime power revisionists. For the Chinese maritime nationalists, Taiwan is also the "unsinkable aircraft carrier," as Gen. Douglas MacArthur once referred to it,[29] located in the heart of maritime Asia with the Luzon Strait to its south, the East China Sea to its north, and the Philippine Sea to its east. The island splits North from Southeast Asia and can be used by the Americans and Japanese to bottle up China's power projection in the first island chain. In geostrategic terms, Taiwan can serve as either a bridgehead for foreign powers to stage attacks on China or a springboard out into the Pacific if controlled by China.[30]

Taiwan merits special attention because it evokes both Chinese imperial thinking and inspires the planning of the nation-state geopolitical thinkers. The island's continued de facto independence is an insult to China's view of itself as a continuous unified civilization and an obstacle to achieving contemporary greatness. Beyond China's desire to keep the empire intact and regain the last holdouts, it wants to change the distribution of power in Asia and is dissatisfied with American dominance.

China, however, is also starting to push out beyond Asia. During the early 21st century, China's energy and commodity companies had to scour the world for natural resources to feed China's economic boom. President Hu Jintao was not ready to rely solely on the US to protect China's global transit and supply lines. With expanding overseas interests, Hu called on the People's Liberation Army Navy (PLAN) to undertake "new historic missions."[31] He began to deploy military forces further afield into the Indian Ocean, the South China Sea, and Indian Ocean and buy and build a set of maritime facilities across the Indian Ocean that could be used as modern-day "coaling" stations and logistics facilities for PLA forces.

China's increased assertiveness during this period was also driven by its hatred of Japan, the only Asian country to have successfully waged war against it. With more naval resources, Hu began to push China's East Asian maritime claims and harass the Japanese-administered Senkaku Islands, reasserting China's primacy.

Under the direction of Xi Jinping, China has continued this muscular foreign policy approach. Xi also has the internal strength that Hu lacked. In recent years, Chinese maritime forces have shifted the balance of power in East Asia's littoral seas. In 2012, Chinese maritime militias and coast guard vessels seized the Scarborough Shoal, an atoll located 100 nautical miles off the Philippine coast, from Manila.

Elsewhere in the South China Sea, Beijing has constructed more than 3,000 acres of manmade military outposts and begun forward deploying missile batteries, drones, and fighter aircraft to these new bases.[32] All the while, Chinese coast guard and fishing fleets continue to harass Filipino, Vietnamese, and Indonesian fishing and coast guard vessels. In the East China Sea, Chinese maritime militias and fishing fleets maintain a regular presence around the Senkaku Islands, over which both Beijing and Tokyo claim sovereignty. Chinese air force activity in Japanese airspace has increased dramatically in the past five years—in 2016 alone, Japan scrambled jets a record 851 times to intercept intruding Chinese fighters.[33]

This strategic behavior is not just about righting the wrongs of the past or reestablishing the empire's boundaries. Indeed, contrary to the official claims of CCP organs, China was never a true maritime power—certainly not in the Qing dynasty and certainly not with a reach into the Pacific. Rather, this type of revisionism is about the dilution of the main contemporary problem: the dominance of US and allied power in the Indo-Pacific.

From a Chinese point of view, the status quo, in which Washington's allies and partners encircle China and form a first island chain running from Japan through Taiwan and the Philippines, is untenable. During peacetime, China still relies on the US to keep the maritime commons open, but during a crisis, the US would potentially constrict China's ability to operate, both commercially and militarily, in the broader oceans. The fact that many of the countries cooperating with the US were once Chinese vassals is a further insult to Chinese feelings. When Foreign Minister Yang Jiechi snapped at an Association of Southeast Asian Nations (ASEAN) forum in Vietnam, "China is a big country and other countries are small countries, and that's just a fact," he was likely referring to both the current power disparity between China and Southeast Asian countries and China's past suzerainty over them.[34]

What is unique about China's revisionism is that the CCP does not appear to be simply using China's imperial past to justify its current territorial claims. Rather, it appears CCP leaders have a deeply held belief in both the real and imagined glory of imperial China.

The CCP highlights the voyages of Ming-era adventurer Zheng He and other Chinese warriors and adventurers to explain the justice of its cause in the South China Sea. It has put out an official white paper explaining its historical rights in the seas.[35] The paper states, "The activities of the Chinese people in the South China Sea date back to over 2,000 years ago. China is the first to have discovered, named, and explored and exploited [the islands of the South China Sea]." China's argument for its claim to the South China Sea may have been soundly repudiated in a 2016 Hague Tribunal ruling, but Beijing still emphasizes its historical rights. Xi does not miss an opportunity to refer to the South China Sea as China's. While some of this is ideological propaganda, meant to justify territorial claims, it would be a mistake to dismiss the very real belief in China in its historical mission to restore quasi-imperial suzerainty.

Revisionism: How Far?

The CCP strategists have to reckon with the truth that America has done more for China's rise than any outside power. It helped China, then the Republic of China, rid itself of Western treaty concessions and gave it a place as one of the five policemen—the great powers who would oversee the international order after World War II. The US granted China a place on the UN Permanent Five and even helped push Russia out of Manchuria. America's uniquely liberal worldview did not try to contain the resurging power of China, now the PRC, but rather offered it a place as a responsible stakeholder in the global liberal system. The fact that China has benefited from US order building has obviated the need for Beijing to challenge the global order thus far.

Still it is the American-led order in Asia that China seeks to revise. China finds the US alliance system threatening, US unofficial support for

Taiwan offensive, and US pushback in maritime East Asia unacceptable. Conversely, China's desire to carve out a sphere of influence in East Asia is antithetical to the US interest in an open economic and political system and a free maritime commons.

In terms of the global order, China's revisionism is constrained by its dependence on the global economic system. From Deng's southern tour in 1992, a move he made to checkmate opponents of reform, through the end of Cold War, a main goal of Chinese diplomacy and economic policy was to reform its economy and join the World Trade Organization. China has strengthened itself as a part of the open international order, and in so doing, it has created dependencies on the US and the West for energy security, technology, and even corporate expertise. It is not yet clear if China wishes to overturn this system or has a workable alternative. It could remain a free rider of the liberal order while establishing hegemony in Asia.

It is not obvious if China has a global strategy in mind. If China were to ally with Russia and Iran—its fellow revisionists—Washington would face a severe challenge to its world order. However, China has not made much strategic effort to either align with Iran or challenge the US position in the Gulf. Rather, it has carefully balanced relations among its main Gulf oil suppliers, Saudi Arabia and Iran. In addition, it has gradually exercised more military power in the region through its Gulf of Aden task force and its basing ambitions in Djibouti.

Eventually, forward-stationed Chinese forces will guard Chinese energy routes, support the ongoing PLAN anti-piracy mission in the Gulf of Aden, and rescue Chinese nationals from conflict zones when needed.[36] However, as of now, China does not yet play much of a role in Middle Eastern geopolitics. China's approach in these areas still serves its interests in building its strength in Asia, its traditional sphere of influence.

As for Russia, the relationship is more complex. The two countries have been uneasy partners and sometimes rivals. Russia was an antagonist in the century of humiliation, a Cold War ally, and then a rival. The two countries almost came to blows in 1969, and China's 1979 invasion of Vietnam had as much to do with challenging Moscow as punishing Hanoi.

Since the end of the Cold War, the two countries have made common cause in diluting US influence through voting patterns on the UN Security Council. They have created the Shanghai Cooperation Organisation to help manage Central Asia. Russia was a major supplier of Chinese military equipment, and the two great powers are finding some commonality in the South China Sea. Nevertheless, Russia will remain suspicious of its more powerful Asian neighbor as it becomes increasingly influential in Central Asia and sends workers into the Russian Far East.

As of now, China's revisionist intentions remain focused on East Asia, the region where it was once dominant and central. In Asia, it has a sense of both what it does not want—US preeminence, US alliances, and a US-style liberal political-economic system—and what it wants—reconsolidation of Qing territory, control over the South China Sea, and a system of deference to its interests. China will face resistance to any hierarchical system; the old tributary states are proud, relatively new independent nations that no longer view China as the exemplar of Confucian moral virtue. China could only get its way through force, economic coercion, and inducements, combined with inattention from the United States.

Toward a US Policy and Strategy

Before fashioning a China strategy, the US must reckon candidly with China's imperial nature. For many reasons, the US has pretended that China under the CCP can become a responsible nation in a liberal international system. But how can it? The CCP runs an empire—this means it demands deference from other Asian nations, is sensitive to any separatism from Taiwan to Hong Kong to Xinjiang, and believes in its civilizational superiority and in the justness of its case.[37] All of this is inconsistent with what the US means when it calls on China to act as a responsible stakeholder.

The US must realize that it is more difficult to deal with an empire than with a "normal" rising power. China turns negotiations over geopolitical disagreements into demands that the restoration of Chinese greatness be respected. For example, US moves to support Taiwan are nonnegotiable for China. From China's view, such efforts signal the United States' intention to split the empire and therefore the unity and stability of China.

If the South China Sea is rightfully a "Chinese lake" and Beijing is simply living out a preordained national destiny, what exactly will China want to discuss? Furthermore, absent US power and presence, the other Asian nations will be treated as lesser vassals, not sovereign equals. Assertive moves by Vietnam or Korea, once vassal states, trigger emotional reactions from China that amplify any geopolitical dispute. China's hatred of Japan is partly the result of the desire to bring low the only Asian power that defeated and humiliated China in war.

However, the fact that China is an empire also provides the US with much more strategic leverage than Washington imagines. This leverage is strengthened by China's structural economic stagnation, which is caused by massive amounts of debt, overcapacity, an inefficient financial system that misallocates capital, slack export markets, and environmental and demographic problems that will cost the CCP significant sums to ameliorate. Nevertheless, Xi's external plans are more, not less, ambitious. He is restructuring the PLA to become a more professional fighting force, pressing China's maritime claims, and enhancing its maritime power, even as he stakes his legacy on his ambitious One Belt, One Road (OBOR) plan to link Asia with Europe.

China now claims or rules territory from the Western approaches to Afghanistan to the top of the South China Sea. That is a massive geography. Moreover, the imperial holdings of Xinjiang, Tibet, and Hong Kong have not gotten any easier to manage. In short, China is in imperial overstretch.[38] A US strategy should begin to take advantage of this.

The US has more at stake in East Asia than Central Asia and as such should focus the hard elements of its strategy on a US buildup in and around the Western Pacific. A much more serious capacity-building effort targeted at the maritime nations of South East Asia and a series of policies that encourage significant economic growth along market lines in these countries would help avert the possibility of China dominating the Western Pacific. The sine qua non of this strategy, however, is rebuilding US military power.

In parallel, China should be encouraged to go west. China will have many land-based investments to defend, and as long as India is consulted closely, doing so will not threaten any conceivable US interest. China should be forced to choose how it spends a shrinking pot of money.

The greatest advantages the US has in such a strategy are its alliances with Japan, South Korea, Australia, and the Philippines and partnerships with Singapore and Taiwan. Partnerships with India, Indonesia, and Vietnam will take time to develop, as each is wary of developing ties that circumscribe their independence. Helping build a US-aligned order consisting of free-market economies, liberal polities, and defense establishments capable of defending their sovereign territory will take time and patience. Nonetheless, the US can and should assist these nations in their quest to become cohesive nation-states capable of protecting their sovereignty and strategic autonomy.

While no one will rush to join a collective security system, much can be done to create greater cohesion among allies and partners. All have a common interest in an Asia free from Chinese hegemony. All share interests in not losing territory and maritime claims to China. All have a military interest in enhanced maritime security. The US is the only country that can put these building blocks together.

The US should support a major military buildup in the region, providing each country with the means to deny China access to its territorial waters and airspace. To do so, Washington must increase the efficacy of its security assistance and arms sales systems. These steps should be backed up with a more active diplomatic effort focused on resolving territorial disputes bilaterally or trilaterally, even as the ASEAN processes go forward. This diplomatic approach will demonstrate that Southeast Asian countries are capable of engaging in international relations and resolving disputes bilaterally, trilaterally, and multilaterally—cooperating where they can. In so doing, a stable order is more likely to develop in Southeast Asia.

Such a strategy in maritime East Asia is intrinsically beneficial to the US. But given China's imperial overstretch, it would also begin to raise questions in Beijing about how much it can afford to compete with the US. The liberal order is open to China and has been since Nixon's presidency. China has the option to forgo costly competition and embed itself more deeply in the liberal order. Certainly, many of China's entrepreneurs would prefer that to territorial grabs, spheres of influence, or the defense of North Korea. If China is surrounded by fully functioning nation-states that embrace free-market economies and are aligned with the US, its global entrepreneurs may press Chinese leaders to change course.

Conclusion

China's revisionism is unique. It is holding onto most of the territories of the Qing Empire and, in that sense, seeks the status quo. However, the unification project is unfinished. Taiwan must come under Chinese political control, Hong Kong must become more of a Chinese vassal, surrounding nations must be more deferential, and the South China Sea should become a Chinese lake. What's more, a more powerful China seeks to undo the American-led security system in Asia. In all these ways, China is revisionist.

China also benefits from the free and open US-led system and the US provision of public goods. Beijing's path to power enmeshed it into a global trading system, thereby constraining some of its strategic options. Accordingly, China does not seem to be seeking hegemony in other regions.

China could still "free ride" on the benefits of the US-led order while acquiring hegemony in Asia. The history of Chinese foreign relations shows the surprising consistency of Sino-centrism. Today, however, Asian elites do not believe that Chinese political culture is superior to their own. Neo-Sinicization will not work, and the PRC's attempts at soft power have had no discernable impact.[39]

Rather, to create a truly Sino-centric system, China would have to rely on economic inducements and military coercion. This strategy would be consistent with China's strategic culture and traditions. Although China's past tributary system did not often require force, its rulers did not hesitate to use violence when they thought it was necessary. And, as noted, China's military modernization over the past two decades has been remarkable, giving it greater capacity to threaten the use of force.

Ultimately, the Qing world order was destroyed because it could not properly analyze and respond to the new geopolitics that were forming in the quickly rising West. China's leaders hold a sense of inevitability regarding their nation's return to primacy. As with the Qing, this could turn out to be a grave mistake. If Washington competes vigorously in the maritime realm while encouraging China to invest more money and diplomatic energy on continental Asia, China will be forced to choose between holding onto its Western empire or advancing its maritime power. A wise strategy would force China to do so while holding out hope that China takes a more productive course in its foreign affairs.

Notes

1. Xi Jinping, "Secure a Decisive Victory in Building a Moderately Prosperous Society in All Respects and Strive for the Great Success of Socialism with Chinese Characteristics for a New Era" (speech, 19th National Congress of the Communist Part of China, October 18, 2017), http://www.xinhuanet.com/english/download/Xi_Jinping's_report_at_19th_CPC_National_Congress.pdf.

2. See, for example, Jane Perlez and Yufan Huang, "Behind China's $1 Trillion Plan to Shake Up the Economic Order," New York Times, May 13, 2017, https://www.nytimes.com/2017/05/13/business/china-railway-one-belt-one-road-1-trillion-plan.html.

3. Lucian W. Pye, "China: Erratic State, Frustrated Society," Foreign Affairs 69, no. 4 (Fall 1990): 56–74, https://www.foreignaffairs.com/articles/asia/1990-09-01/china-erratic-state-frustrated-society.

4. Henry Kissinger, On China (New York: Penguin Books, 2011), 16–22.

5. Shivshankar Menon, "How China Buked Western Expectations and What It Means for World Order," Brookings Institution, March 10, 2016, https://www.brookings.edu/blog/order-from-chaos/2016/03/10/how-china-bucked-western-expectations-and-what-it-means-for-world-order/.

6. National Committee on US-China Relations, "Full Text from President Xi Jinping's Speech," https://www.ncuscr.org/content/full-text-president-xi-jinpings-speech.

7. Peter C. Perdue, "The Tenacious Tributary System," Journal of Contemporary China 24, no. 96 (May 2015): 1002–14, http://www.tandfonline.com/doi/abs/10.1080/10670564.2015.1030949.

8. Pamela Kyle Crossley, The Manchus (Cambridge, MA: Wiley-Blackwell, 2002).

9. John K. Fairbank, The Chinese World Order: Traditional China's Foreign Relations (Cambridge, MA: Harvard University Press, 1968), 3.

10. Perdue, "The Tenacious Tributary System."

11. Odd Arne Westad, Restless Empire: China and the World Since 1750 (New York: Basic Books, 2012), 8.

12. Charles Patterson Giersch, Asian Borderlands: The Transformation of Qing China's Yunnan Frontier (Cambridge, MA: Harvard University Press, 2006).

13. Jonathan D. Spence, The Search for Modern China, 3rd ed. (New York: W. W. Norton, 2012), 117.

14. David E. Mungello, The Great Encounter of China and the West, 1500–1800, 4th ed. (Lanham, MD: Rowman & Littlefield Publishers, 2012).

15. Emperor Qianlong, "Letter to King George, 1793," in World History: Patterns of Interaction, http://farwell.glk12.org/pluginfile.php/22026/mod_resource/content/1/Letter%20to%20King%20George%20III%201793.pdf.

16. Matt Schiavenza, "How Humiliation Drove Modern Chinese History," Atlantic, October 25, 2013, https://www.theatlantic.com/china/archive/2013/10/how-humiliation-drove-modern-chinese-history/280878/.

17. William C. Kirby, "The Internationalization of China: Foreign Relations at Home and Abroad in the Republican Era," China Quarterly, no. 150 (June 1997): 433–58, http://www.jstor.org/stable/655344.

18. Stanislav Myšička, "Chinese Support for Communist Insurgencies in Southeast Asia During the Cold War," *International Journal of Chinese Studies* 6, no. 3 (December 2015): 203–30, https://www.um.edu.my/docs/default-source/ics/ics-ijcs/full-issue-6-3.pdf.

19. Jon Halliday and Jung Chang, *Mao: The Unknown Story* (New York: Knopf, 2005), 549.

20. Ministry of Foreign Affairs of the People's Republic of China, "A Policy of 'One Country, Two Systems,' on Taiwan," http://www.fmprc.gov.cn/mfa_eng/ziliao_665539/3602_665543/3604_665547/t18027.shtml.

21. Tony Capaccio, "China Has World's Most Active Missile Program: US," *Sydney Morning Herald*, July 11, 2013, http://www.smh.com.au/world/china-has-worlds-most-active-missile-program-us-20130711-2prnr.html.

22. Jeremy Bender, "Pentagon Report: Chinese Ballistic Missiles Can Target Nearly the Entirety of the US," *Business Insider*, May 11, 2015, http://www.businessinsider.com/chinese-missiles-can-hit-entirety-of-us-2015-5.

23. US Naval Institute, "Document: Pentagon Ballistic and Cruise Missile Threat Report," June 27, 2017, https://news.usni.org/2017/06/27/document-pentagon-ballistic-and-cruise-missile-threat.

24. Eric Heginbotham et al., *The U.S.-China Military Scorecard: Forces, Geography, and the Evolving Balance of Power, 1996–2017* (Santa Monica, CA: Rand Corporation, 2015), 30, https://www.rand.org/pubs/research_reports/RR392.html.

25. Andrew Browne, "Beijing Reaches for Military Upper Hand in Asia," *Wall Street Journal*, October 21, 2015, https://www.wsj.com/articles/beijing-reaches-for-military-upper-hand-in-asia-1445318222.

26. Minnie Chan, "China Has Started Building Its Third Aircraft Carrier, Military Sources Say," *South China Morning Post*, January 4, 2018, http://www.scmp.com/news/china/diplomacy-defence/article/2126883/china-has-started-building-its-third-aircraft-carrier.

27. Ronald O'Rourke, *China Naval Modernization: Implications for U.S. Navy Capabilities—Background and Issue for Congress*, Congressional Research Service, December 13, 2017, https://fas.org/sgp/crs/row/RL33153.pdf.

28. See, for example, Josh Chin and Liza Lin, "China's All-Seeing Surveillance State Is Reading Its Citizens' Faces," *Wall Street Journal*, June 26, 2017, https://www.wsj.com/articles/the-all-seeing-surveillance-state-feared-in-the-west-is-a-reality-in-china-1498493020.

29. Douglas MacArthur, "Draft Memorandum: General MacArthur's Message on Formosa," Harry S. Truman Presidential Library and Museum, August 17, 1950, https://www.trumanlibrary.org/whistlestop/study_collections/achesonmemos/view.php?documentVersion=both&documentYear=1950&documentid=67-4_25.

30. Alan M. Wachman, *Why Taiwan? Geostrategic Rationales for China's Territorial Integrity* (Stanford, CA: Stanford University Press, 2007).

31. Daniel M. Hartnett, "The 'New Historic Missions': Reflections on Hu Jintao's Military Legacy," in *Assessing the People's Liberation Army in the Hu Jintao Era*, ed. Roy Kamphausen, David Lai, and Travis Tanner (Carlisle Barracks, PA: United States Army War College Press, 2014), 31–80.

32. Tom Phillips, "Images Show 'Significant' Chinese Weapons Systems in South

China Sea," *Guardian*, December 15, 2016, https://www.theguardian.com/world/2016/dec/15/images-show-significant-chinese-weapons-systems-in-south-china-sea.

33. Jesse Johnson, "Japan's Fighter Jet Scrambles Set New Record in 2016 amid Surging Chinese Military Activity," *Japan Times*, April 4, 2017, http://www.japantimes.co.jp/news/2017/04/14/national/japans-fighter-jet-scrambles-set-new-record-2016-amid-surging-chinese-military-activity/.

34. John Pomfret, "U.S. Takes a Tougher Tone with China," *Washington Post*, June 30, 2010, http://www.washingtonpost.com/wp-dyn/content/article/2010/07/29/AR2010072906416.html.

35. State Council Information Office of the People's Republic of China, "China Adheres to the Position of Settling Through Negotiation the Relevant Disputes Between China and the Philippines in the South China Sea," July 13, 2016, http://english.gov.cn/state_council/ministries/2016/07/13/content_281475392503075.htm.

36. The PLA has already been called into action on several occasions to protect overseas Chinese. In 2011, PLA assets aided the evacuation of 35,000 Chinese citizens from Libya as violence swept the country. Then in 2015, the PLAN evacuated 570 Chinese citizens from two port cities in Yemen. See Reuters, "China Says Completes Evacuation of Its Nationals from Yemen," March 31, 2015, http://www.reuters.com/article/us-yemen-security-china-idUSKBN0MR0B420150331; and Mathieu Duchâtel, Oliver Bräuner, and Zhou Hang, *Protesting China's Overseas Interests* (Solna, Sweden: Stockholm International Peace Research Institute, 2014).

37. Frank N. Pieke, "From Empire to Nation, or Why Taiwan, Tibet and Xinjiang Will Not Be Given Independence," in *Knowing China: A Twenty-First Century Guide* (Cambridge, UK: Cambridge University Press), 121–43.

38. For a comprehensive discussion of imperial overstretch, see Paul Kennedy, *The Rise and Fall of Great Powers: Economic Change and Military Conflict from 1500 to 2000* (New York: Random House, 1987).

39. Zachary Keck, "Destined to Fail: China's Soft Power Push," *Diplomat*, January 7, 2013, http://thediplomat.com/2013/01/destined-to-fail-chinas-soft-power-offensive/.

3

Iran:
The Shi'ite Imperial Power

REUEL MARC GERECHT

The sectarian wars in Iraq and Syria have fundamentally changed the Islamic Republic. They have become arenas for a new militant Shi'ite solidarity that has crossed the Arab-Persian divide: Iranian-led, non-Iranian militias, thousands strong, now fight in foreign lands. Not that long ago an academic consensus on the Islamic Republic told us that the mullahs could no longer generate the kind of religious allegiance to send Iranians, let alone non-Iranian Shi'ites, into combat far from home. If the Islamic Revolution was not completely out of gas, it certainly had lost its mojo. The idea that Iran was becoming a revolutionary Shi'ite imperial power would have seemed far-fetched.

The Islamic Republic now resembles the Soviet Union of 1979: a police state, incapable of reforming itself while drowning in corruption, expanding abroad to protect the nation and its "faith." But unlike the USSR, which in the end just had Marx's and Lenin's desiccated shibboleths to sustain an empire, the Islamic Republic has a still vibrant Shi'ite identity. It is the only idea, mixed with revolutionary intent, that the mullahs and their praetorians, the Revolutionary Guards, can lock onto that can motivate the faithful and undermine critics who stopped believing in the cleric-constructed Islamic state.

Ecumenicalism vs. Sectarianism

Tehran can imagine a Middle East without the United States. The clerical regime quickly adapted to and exploited the American invasion of and withdrawal from Iraq. Both shocked and excited by the Great Arab Revolt in Tunisia and Egypt in 2010–11, and horrified when the rebellion hit Syria a year later, the mullahs have worked hard to turn instability to their advantage.

Unappreciated by Western observers, the pro-democracy Green Movement, which rallied millions of Iranians into street demonstrations in 2009 over a contested presidential election, also primed the regime for more outward expansion. The Green Revolt devastated what was left of the regime's legitimacy, especially among the young and bazaaris, who had seen mullah-controlled foundations, such as the gargantuan *owqaf* religious trusts, and the Revolutionary Guards' vast business empire eat away at their commerce and social status. Denied legitimacy at home, the clerical regime looked beyond its borders. Endangered Shi'ites became a new cause, both an excuse and a heartfelt mission for an Iranian elite itching to establish a new order.

Qasem Soleimani, the leader of the Revolutionary Guards' expeditionary outfit, the Quds Force, and the supreme commander of all of Iran's foreign militias, has become a social media paladin for the regime. His pictures on the front lines of the empire are signposts of Iran's new humanitarian, "anti-terrorist" mission. He is, as his brother proudly put it, "born in our family, but he doesn't belong to us, he belongs to the country and to the Shiites."[1]

Although one may question whether all the Arabs, Afghans, and Pakistanis fighting for the Islamic Republic have done so because of militant Shi'ite fraternity, such a force could not take shape, let alone be used in the ghastly combat in Syria, unless its esprit were solid. No other Muslim state— not the pan-Arabists of yesteryear or the ever-proselytizing, super-rich Saudis—has been able to accomplish this trick in the modern era.

Until recently, the Islamic Republic had only organized and inspired the Lebanese Hezbollah, the first and favorite foreign child of the Islamic Revolution. Indeed, until the Anglo-American invasion of Iraq in 2003, Tehran actually preferred outreach more focused on Sunnis. Before the revolution in 1979, the Palestine Liberation Organization gave Khomeini's followers paramilitary training. After the revolution, the ruling mullahs and the Revolutionary Guards saw themselves as the vanguard of an Islamic Revolution that would one day sweep away the Westernized elites of the Middle East.

The ultimate believer in soft power, Khomeini really did think the downfall of the shah could set off a chain reaction among Muslims, Sunni and Shi'ite alike. After the Iran-Iraq War (1980–88) ended in a devastating Iranian defeat, the clerical regime still dreamed of an anti-American realignment among Muslim countries, offering its support to Sunni Muslims willing to emphasize their anti-Americanism and anti-Zionism more than their anti-Shi'ism. Ali Akbar Hashemi-Rafsanjani, who became speaker of Iran's parliament (1980–89) and then president (1989–97), and his aide-de-camp Hassan Rouhani excelled at organizing ecumenical gatherings of anti-American Sunni Muslims.

And what the regime conducted publicly it also proselytized clandestinely: The Ministry of Intelligence and the Guards began organizing paramilitary training programs and weapon deliveries to Sunnis willing to oppose American, Israeli, and Arab enemies. Such ecumenical militancy probably reached its apex when, according to the 9/11 Commission Report, the Sudanese leader Hassan at-Turabi, who also thought Sunnis and Shi'ites should cooperate against common foes, orchestrated contact between al Qaeda and Iran.[2]

The Iranian revolution's ecumenical intent still lives on. The regime's fundamental *mission civilisatrice* is inextricably attached to the idea that the Islamic Republic is on the cutting edge of showing *all* Muslims how Islamists can run a modern state without forsaking the faith and their resistance to the West. Yet Tehran has now embraced sectarian warfare as *the* means to expand its influence on the ground.

The evolution from ecumenicalism to Shi'ite imperialism likely was not done initially with much forethought. The über-Shi'ite option abroad was surely chosen at first by default. The fall of Saddam Hussein and Baghdad's Sunni ruling class in 2003 freed the Iraqi Shi'a, who account for at least 60 percent of the country's population. The irredentist Sunni insurgency against the Americans, which quickly mutated into ferocious attacks against Shi'ites, and the US military's failure to break this insurgency in its infancy opened the door to savage sectarianism and the Islamic Republic.

The clerical regime intervened decisively. Tehran increased aid to well-established Shi'ite organizations that had taken refuge in Iran during Saddam's rule and, more importantly, also threw its support to militant, homegrown Shi'ite groups, such as the Sadrists, willing to attack US forces. In this period—2004 to 2006—Tehran realized it could create effective

Hezbollah-like militias well anchored inside Shi'ite Iraq. Once the Islamic Republic Supreme Leader Ali Khamenei saw how hesitant the United States was, how it seemed incapable of suppressing the insurgency, the temptation to make Americans bleed was seemingly irresistible. Besieged by Sunnis who adopted evermore vicious tactics, the Iraqi Shi'a community, which historically had intimate but often distrustful relations with Iran, had nowhere else to turn for support but to Tehran—especially once the Iraqi Shi'ite establishment realized the Americans were leaving.

The Syrian rebellion in 2012 against the regime of Bashar al Assad, a secular tyrant from a small heretical Shi'ite clan, the Alawites, further cemented into place this new approach to Shi'ite solidarity. The mullahs could not afford to lose their ally in Damascus without risking the Lebanese Hezbollah. Since the clerical regime created the Hezbollah in the early 1980s, Alawites have reliably funneled Iranian weaponry and supplies into Lebanon. A Sunni victory in Damascus would have signaled Iranian weakness throughout the region, especially in the Levant, where a Syrian Sunni victory might reanimate the downtrodden Lebanese Sunnis and throw into question Hezbollah's dominance. A Syrian Sunni victory would have also strengthened the spine of Iraqi Sunnis, who obviously remain opposed to Shi'ite supremacy.

Brigadier General Hosein Hamedani, who had operational control of the Revolutionary Guard's expeditionary Quds Force in Syria, led the effort to create and direct these new units. Before he died in the battle for Aleppo in October 2015, he gave a revealing interview on how important the Syrian war effort was to the Islamic Republic and how critical the creation of militias was to frontline combat and regime survival. For him, the Levant and Iraq are holy ground where "100,000 [special] individuals from our divine prophetic history are buried."[3] And so earthly politics intertwine with religion. "The enemy hasn't come to destroy the Syrian Baath Party," the general tells us, referring to the political party through which the Assad family officially rules. The Americans "themselves tell us they've intervened to cut short Iranian influence, to weaken the [Lebanese] Hezbollah, and, the ultimate objective, to guarantee the security of Israel. . . . Syria is the key region [in the Middle East]. In comparison to Iraq, Lebanon, and Yemen, Syria is the most important . . . it is in Syria, where our interests can most be hurt. . . . To protect the accomplishments of the Islamic revolution, we had to intervene."[4]

In recognizing his achievement, the Guards published a tribute, *1600 Hours* [4:00 p.m.] *in Aleppo*, in which Hamedani is the "master of the asymmetrical wars of the resistance axis."[5] Where once the "resistance" would have been synonymous with the clerical regime's opposition to the United States and Israel, it now includes Sunni Arabs, too, who have allied themselves violently against Assad and the Shi'ite government in Baghdad. Iranian propaganda frequently describes the Islamic State, like its predecessor, the Shi'ite-killing al Qaeda in Iraq of Abu Musab az-Zarqawi, as an organization that sprang from American and Zionist conspiracies. *1600 Hours* creates a seamless history for the general, who was the lead officer in crushing the pro-democracy Green Movement, from his combat in the Iran-Iraq conflict through his battles in Syria. On both the home front and abroad, Hamedani was on the cutting edge of why and how the clerical regime adopted Shi'ite imperialism as the vehicle to ensure the Islamic Revolution's survival.

Shi'ite Solidarity, Shi'ite Vengeance

The wars in Syria and Iraq play powerfully on long-standing Muslim sentiments. Modern Iranians and Arabs—those educated to think of themselves in nationalist terms and even many who are deeply religious but still cherish an inclusive Islamic identity—often dislike talking about the divisions within the faith. Perhaps because of the violent convulsions in early Islamic history, where the fear of *fitna*—a seditious fracture among believers—became seared into the collective memory of Muslims, even the most anti-Shi'ite Sunni or anti-Sunni Shi'ite may pause in expressing his antipathy before nonbelievers.

Yet Shi'ites and Sunnis, even among the secular, usually have an acute sense for recognizing who each other are. And all Shi'ites, except those who have been raised in the West and in Iran, are conscious of their historic political inferiority. The unspeakable savagery of Saddam's regime against the Shi'a, the ferocity of the post-Saddam internecine strife, and the ugly sideshow in Yemen, where Houthi Shi'ites clash with native Sunnis and Saudis, and blood-soaked Syria have turned the Sunni-Shi'ite divide into the biggest fault line in the Middle East.

Unlike militant Islamic ecumenicalism, Shi'ite chauvinism has running room inside Iranian society. The failures of the Islamic Revolution—the oppression that climaxed in 2009 and 2010 when the Iranian elite turned on itself and started torturing the children of those who had made the revolution—have made Islamism an increasingly hard sale. The enormous intellectual vibrancy of Iranian society in the 1990s—the open discussion of the virtues and the sins of Western societies and the despotism of the Islamic Republic—had by 2010 died.[6] It is impossible to overstate how intellectually arid Iranian culture has become in comparison to the heady days of the 1990s when many college-educated Iranians, including some clerics, believed a smooth transition from Khomeinism to something softer and more democratic was possible. Many Iranians wanted a hybrid society that proudly mixed Western and Islamic Persian ideals. This optimism could also be seen among Western journalists, scholars, and diplomats who then covered Iran.[7]

But the pull of Shi'ism is something else. Although it is difficult to quantify, the Shi'ite content of Iranian internal propaganda has definitely increased in the past decade. This partly reflects the increasing importance of the Basij, the "mobilization" corps under the control of the Revolutionary Guards, which monitors, polices, and, at least in the eyes of the state, inspires Iranian society. The Basij mostly come from the non-college-educated base of the regime, the "urban peasants" who rally to the revolution whenever demonstrations are called for. Former President Mahmoud Ahmadinejad (2005–13) came from this lower-class milieu, and his Shi'ism was exuberantly popular.

As the old Islamic Republic has waned, as the first-generation revolutionaries have grown old and become associated with rampant corruption or even joined the opposition, revolutionary rhetoric has calcified. It is not just the college educated who have grown bored with Mercedes-driving, uncharismatic mullahs preaching virtue. Anticlericalism, always a stable of Persian poets and humor, is today a serious concern for mullahs who fear the increasing distance between the clergy and the working class. We have seen a precipitous drop in the number of Iranian men willing to become seminarians even though that remains the route to power in the Islamic Republic.[8]

The mullahs know they have lost the college educated. The Green Movement, which brought between two to three million people onto the streets of Tehran, is irrefutable evidence that theocracy does not sit well with those who have received Westernized educations.[9] Since the revolution, university enrollment has skyrocketed (though academic standards have declined), leaving the regime with a seemingly intractable problem: It has educated millions in universities that, despite innumerable "reforms," Islamize poorly.[10]

The great unknown in Iran is the depth of regime support among the urban poor. Twenty-five years ago, Ayatollah Mohammad-Reza Mahdavi-Kani, a prominent conservative mullah, a mainstay of the theocracy, openly worried whether regime clerics who made every political issue religious, who were quick to condemn opponents as "enemies of God," were rendering the holy law meaningless and destroying Islam. He was concerned that an explicitly religious regime was secularizing Iranian society through the excesses of a state-enforced faith. The nationwide anti-regime demonstrations that erupted in December 2017, which may have been spearheaded by the non-college-educated, suggest that the regime is in deep trouble with the provincial "urban peasantry," too.

The secularization of Iranian society has been a favorite theme of French observers of the Islamic Republic, who are always attentive to the friction between church and state. Their focus is undoubtedly warranted: First-rank intellectuals, both lay and clerical, have produced fine—in the Muslim Middle East, unparalleled—critiques of theocracy and popular sovereignty. Some of these men—Khomeini's "defrocked" successor Ali Montazeri, Abd al-Karim Soroush, Mohsen Kadivar, Mohammad Mojtahed Shabestari, Hasan Yusofi Eshkevari, and, in his own bumbling, contradictory way, former President Mohammad Khatami—have become known in the West. (Soroush and Kadivar both live in exile in the United States.) Many more have gone to ground in the Islamic Republic, waiting perhaps for another opportunity to speak their minds without fear of imprisonment and torture.

We do not know how much the Islamic Republic has degraded or depoliticized the people's attachment to their faith. We do know that mosque attendance has plummeted. In 2015 a Revolutionary Guard commander, Zia Eddin Hozni, revealed that only about 3,000 of the country's 57,000 Shi'ite mosques were fully operational—and of the 3,000 some were only functioning during the religious months of Ramadan and Muharram.[11]

The Shi'a have usually been less diligent than Sunnis in mosque attendance, but it is striking that in an explicitly Shi'ite state run by mullahs, the faithful are staying away in such numbers. We can make educated guesses that a cleric-lite religion has become much more popular. Since the fall of Saddam in 2003, the popularity in Iran of Grand Ayatollah Ali Sistani, the preeminent cleric of Iraq who is Iranian by birth, has exponentially increased. That rise is undoubtedly in part a reflection of his strong preference for clerics keeping a certain distance from government, which is a rebuke of Khomeini's innovative *velayat-e faqih*, or "the rule of the jurisconsult." Sistani's carefulness about seeing Iranian officials and the suspicions he expresses, via his aides, about Tehran's intentions in Iraq also are well-known among both Iranians and Iraqis. Inside the Islamic Republic, we also know that "peasant Shi'ism," which is ritual-heavy and mystical, has not been hurt by the revolution, probably in great part because of its ambivalent and ambiguous relationship with mullahs, who have often been viewed by Iranians as acquisitive and licentious.

It is not unreasonable to surmise that part of Ahmadinejad's considerable lower-class appeal was his skepticism about clerical Shi'ism, which by the end of his presidency became an open dismissiveness toward the politicized clergy, even Khamenei himself. This "democratized" Shi'ism eventually doomed Ahmadinejad with the supreme leader and other powerful mullahs.

Shi'ite Islam, with all its mysticism and historical magic men, may remain as strong an identity inside Iran as it was at the revolution. What has changed is how Iranians filter the faith through the clergy. What Eshkevari, a cleric, said in 2000 in Berlin, before he was arrested in Iran, sentenced to death for apostasy, and then just imprisoned, is certainly still true: "We can say clearly that the conflict between Islam and Western modernity is the most critical and crucial problem that the Muslim world has confronted in the past 550 years. It is so grave that the destiny of Muslim societies depend on finding a way out from this conflict."[12]

Today the corruption, the clerical arrogance, and the regime's nastiness have either concluded this debate in favor of the West or made this once-primal question a contretemps. Many Iranians may still have a problem with the West, especially the United States, but the omnipresent, oppressive hand of the regime and the increasing staleness of society have made anti-Western propaganda much less compelling. The United States is far away; the clerical regime is at the front door.

Iranian imperialism today plays on the complexity of the country's internal and shifting allegiances. Preaching about Iran liberating the mostly Sunni Muslim world from the yoke of the United States and Westernized native oppressors simply does not ring true when Sunnis have largely sat on the sidelines, encouraged, or actively participated in the slaughter of Shi'ites. It does not ring true when Islamic universalism at home is often rhetorical camouflage for government incompetence. The base of the Iranian regime today—unlike at the time of the revolution, when the muscle and dynamism belonged to the university educated who had blended Islam and Marxism into a convulsive cocktail—are the less-educated faithful who ardently feel their Shi'ite identity and inextricably and effortlessly mix their religious commitment with their Persian pride. The Islamic Republic's ruling elite has understandably fallen back on the country's inner themes as revolutionary dogma has lost its appeal.

This approach probably has some traction even with Iranians who hate the regime. During the Green Movement protests, the demonstrators famously mocked many of the holies of the Islamic Revolution. *"Na Ghazeh, Na Lobnan, janam feda-ye Iran"* [Not for Gaza, not for Lebanon, I sacrifice my life only for Iran] was a popular protest chant. Given the re-eruption of this chant and many others aimed at the mullahs' foreign adventures in the December 2017 demonstrations, Iranian youth do not appear wild about the clerical regime's war in Syria, its machinations in Iraq, and its clandestine weapons deliveries to the Houthis in Yemen. Iranian social media certainly reveals unease among Tehran's college-educated with the regime's policy in Syria, or as one brave student put it in person to the Second Deputy Speaker of Parliament Ali Motahari: "Are we on the right side in Syria? . . . We are definitely guilty before the tearful eyes of Syrian children."[13]

But it is, nevertheless, tricky for Iranians to mock the regime's commitment to defending Shi'ites (even dubious ones like the Alawites) who are being challenged by Sunnis. The eruption of the Islamic State, even though the clerical regime and its sectarian machinations fertilized the ground for its birth, has made it easier for the mullahs to play the Sunni terrorist card in domestic politics. The theocracy's constant propaganda— that Iran is the only thing standing in the way of a broader Middle Eastern implosion—appears to have influenced Iranian dissidents, even those ardently opposed to the mullahs. Akbar Ganji, the former Revolutionary

Guardsman turned journalist turned Iran's most famous imprisoned dissident turned exile, is monomaniacal on this theme of Iran as an island of stability. And he has excused Tehran's complicity in the death of hundreds of thousands of Syrian Sunnis, preferring to blame everyone, including the United States and Israel.[14]

Other Iranian exiles who actually focus on human rights have been more forthcoming, but it is still striking, given the massive destruction that Iran and its allies have wrought in Syria, how few, brief, and equivocating these condemnations are. The Obama administration's obvious hope that Iranian casualties would mount sufficiently in Syria to cause disquiet at home never made much sense among the revolutionary set, especially younger Guards who finally have found an opportunity to show their fidelity and bravery as their fathers showed theirs against Saddam. The death toll among them in Syria since January 2012 is around 500, an easily sustainable loss rate for a 125,000-man corps, which rotates both Quds Force and mainline officers and soldiers regularly through Syria.[15]

Social media reveals some anxiety among college-educated Iranians about Iranian deaths in Syria. But such views and emotions appear sporadically, perhaps because the regime so efficiently silences them. Dissent on Syria, Iraq, Lebanon, and Yemen appears to be far from developing into a movement. Publicly siding against Shi'ites in favor of Sunnis can be an arduous existential exercise for Iranians.

Lasting Scars

There is no good historical parallel for today's sectarian clash in the 1,350 years of tension between the shi'atu Ali, or the party of Ali—that is, those who believe rightful rule belonged to the prophet's family via his cousin and son-in-law Ali bin Abi Talib—and the Sunna, or those who have recognized as legitimate whoever holds "the reins of power" (ulu'ul-amr). Once upon a time, in the formative period of Islamic history, the Sunni-Shi'ite clash was about an elemental conception of salvation: If Muslims followed errant leaders, then the community as a whole could be damned.[16] As the idea of salvation in Islam became more individualized and less communitarian, the Shi'ite-Sunni rivalry became less intense though remained omnipresent.

Shi'ism became an escape route for all forms of heterodoxy. The long battle between the Sunni Ottomans and the Shi'ite Safavids, which had been the fiercest clash between Sunnis and Shi'ites in Islamic history, never produced the level of barbarism that has become routine in the 21st century.

And given the death toll and destruction in the Sunni insurrection against the Assad dictatorship, Sunni antipathy for Arab and Iranian Shi'ites is unlikely to diminish for decades. Somewhere around 500,000 people have likely died in this conflict, the majority of whom are Sunni civilians slaughtered by the regime and its allies. Around five million Syrians, again mostly Sunni, have become refugees abroad, and perhaps as many as seven million people have been internally displaced.[17] Vast tracks of Sunni Syria, especially the oldest, richest, and largest city of the country, Aleppo, which anchored Syrian Sunni society, have been devastated.

Syria and Iraq are the historical heartland of the Sunni Arab identity: The Umayyad (661–750) and Abbasid (750–1258) caliphs reigned in Damascus and Baghdad, respectively. Shi'ites challenged both dynasties. In both cities, Shi'ites now rule, and Sunnis bow down or risk their lives. It is impossible to overstate how galling this is to the Arab Sunni consciousness.

Assad's Alawite regime would have fallen if it had not been for the military and financial aid that Tehran extended. Not long ago, both Iranian and Iraqi mullahs, who come from the "Twelver" branch of Shi'ism and represent the vast majority of Shi'ites, treated the Alawites as beyond the pale. The Iranian-regime clergy has now officially recognized them as canonically acceptable. For both Shi'ites and Sunnis, the war in Syria has fundamentally changed once-cherished conceptions of the sacred and the profane.

And Iran's mullahs have undoubtedly done the math: In the classical Middle East—from Egypt through the Persian Gulf and from the Levant to Afghanistan—Sunnis and Shi'ites are roughly even in number. Although the Islamic Republic still conducts cultural and religious missions among non-Arab Sunni Muslims, its focus has always been squarely on its own neighborhood and overwhelmingly on the Arabs. Sectarian politics make excellent tactical sense since possible Arab Sunni coalitions against Iran have no cohesive military power, have little expeditionary capacity, and inevitably will default back to supporting radical Sunni groups, which are the only armed force capable of making the Iranians and their allies bleed. This Sunni extremist temptation, of course, further cements the Islamic Republic's centripetal position among the Arab Shi'a.

No Sunni Arab force has put boots on the ground in defense of its religious brethren in Syria and Iraq. Egypt, the only Sunni Arab state that could conceivably deploy an expeditionary ground force if someone else supplied the transport and logistics, refused to fight the Saudis' war in Yemen. In Syria, Abd al-Fattah as-Sissi, field marshal turned president for life, has come out in favor of Assad. He even deployed a small, symbolic force to Syria on Assad's side. In Yemen, the Saudis and the Emirates, with overwhelming air power, have probably managed to make a bad situation worse, proving that their battlefield incompetence is matched by their strategic inability to exploit the differences within the Houthi community and, more importantly, recognize the permanence of Houthi power in northern Yemen.

Saudi actions, more than any preexisting ideological affinity between the Houthis and the Iranians, have likely gained Tehran a permanent foothold in the peninsula. Imagining the Revolutionary Guards building a Yemeni version of the Hezbollah is now not unthinkable. Yemeni militancy on the Sunni side, which has produced one of the most lethal branches of al Qaeda, could see a much more organized Shi'ite twin capable of abetting Iranian efforts to radicalize and organize the Saudi Shi'a, the ultimate prize.

The Middle East has essentially reverted to where it had been from the 10th century to 1918: Just two peoples—the Turks and the Iranians—can dominate the region. And unlike the past, where Turkish warriors usually held the high ground, today the Turkish Republic has no stomach for wars much beyond its borders. That leaves the Iranians versus the (Sunni) Arabs.

No one in the Middle East believes that the advanced Western weaponry in Gulf Arab armies has made these states capable of checkmating Iranian designs. They may not be paper tigers when guarding their own borders, but they have no capacity to project power. Once the Iranians start to load up with advanced conventional Russian hardware, which they can commence in under four years according to United Nations Security Council Resolution 2231, Gulf Arab self-confidence will undoubtedly be shaken.[18]

Even before the Great Arab Revolt convulsed the region, the secular Arab-state Middle East was dying, and Shi'ite and Sunni Islamists were the only ones creatively and aggressively imagining the future. All Shi'ites can find some passionate common ground in how much they loathe the Shi'ite-hating Wahhabis and the Gulf princes who indulge them. The Iranians probably have not been the catalyst for the rising violence in Bahrain, but they have surely done what they can to encourage Shi'ite insurrection.

Although the United States has come to think of the Saudis as a permanent fixture of the Middle East, it is doubtful that the Iranians view the family as immovable. Saudi Arabia and Bahrain oppress the largest number of Arab Shi'ites in the Middle East. If the ruling Sunni families of Bahrain and Saudi Arabia could be upended and the Shi'a in the oil-rich Eastern Province and Bahrain freed, the Middle East would be transformed. Only the United States' military might—the perception in the Middle East that Washington will use its armed forces to check Iranian adventurism—keeps the southern Middle East from becoming unhinged.

Iranian Advantages

The Russians, too, have done the math. Iran has never posed a strategic threat to Moscow. The Islamic Republic has never gained a foothold in the Caucasus and Central Asia outside of Tajikistan, the only Persian-speaking country in the former Soviet Union. And even in Tajikistan, anti-Iranian sentiments are widespread. The Islamic Republic's cultural and religious outreach to the region has flopped, thwarted by the Sunni-Shi'ite divide (the vast majority of Central Asian Muslims are Sunni), Iranian cultural arrogance, and the superior efforts of Turkish Gülenists, Saudis, and other Sunni missionaries.

Vladimir Putin has already calculated that his own brutal actions toward Sunni Muslims in the Caucasus and his support of ferociously anti-Islamist rulers in the former Soviet Union do not have a prohibitive downside. He does not seem to fear Sunni Islamic radicalism in Russia: Whatever anti-Russian designs the Islamic State or al Qaeda may have, they have so far failed to launch major terrorist operations inside the Russian police state. Putin's alliance with Shi'ite Iran is a logical extension of this domestic self-confidence; it is also a smart strategic move since Iranian power has no effective Arab counterweight. The closer Russia is to the Islamic Republic, the more the Arab states, particularly oil-rich Gulf states, must treat Russia with greater respect and deference.

Tehran is set to become the largest single client for Russian military hardware. Moscow finally delivered to Tehran S-300 antiaircraft missiles, which have certainly complicated any Israeli threat to the clerical regime's nuclear sites. The Russian-Iranian axis has become militarily dominant in the northern Middle East. The Syrian refugee maelstrom, which Iran and Russia in part provoked, has worked brilliantly for Putin, further destabilizing the European Union.

And spiritually, on the most important issue, Russia and Iran are a pair: Russian propaganda against America's insidious efforts to spread its values in the Russian realm, undermining traditional culture and the mores of the Russian Orthodox church, is remarkably similar to Khamenei's gravamen against the morally corrupting soft-power machinations of the United States. Unlike the Soviet Union, Russia does not pose an ideological temptation for Iranian youth and intellectuals. Iranian Shi'ite imperialism dovetails nicely with Putin's great power ambitions.

And the United States is in an extraordinarily difficult position to counter, let alone roll back, Iranian influence and military adventures, at least in the northern Middle East. The Joint Comprehensive Plan of Action (JCPOA) has put Washington into a surreal situation: The nuclear deal funds Iranian expansion. The crux of that accord is to trade commerce for (temporary) nuclear restraint. The Obama administration fully understood this conundrum, which is why the president and those charged to sell the agreement highlighted the politically "moderating" potential of the JCPOA and Iran's domestic economic demands, as if the Islamic Republic were a Western democracy inclined to take from the military and give to the commonwealth.[19] Open-source information already shows a 24 percent increase in the Revolutionary Guard Corps budget for 2017–18.[20]

President Barack Obama believed the United States was overextended in the Middle East. For him, Washington had no major national security interests in Iraq, Syria, Lebanon, or Yemen that warranted risking nuclear diplomacy with Tehran. In effect Obama ceded those countries to Iranian mischief and possible control.

The president certainly understood that the mullahs were spreading sectarian strife across the region (he repeatedly said so), but either he did not believe the harm done transcended the benefit of punting the nuclear question down the road or he hoped the accord would economically transform the Iranian regime, by making the so-called moderate faction behind Rouhani politically dominant or the "hardline" faction behind the Revolutionary Guards less malign. Or he did not really care since he no longer wanted the United States to be a hegemonic power in the region. Those really are the only possibilities.

We already know the atomic accord has not moderated the Revolutionary Guards. A quick read of Rouhani's speeches and books, or a review of the Islamic Republic's economic and foreign policies in the 1990s, should have told Obama and intelligence analysts, who remain addicted to the "Rouhani is a moderate" meme, that tens of billions of dollars' worth of trade with Europe and Asia in the 1990s failed to moderate Iran's foreign policy, its campaigns of bombings and assassinations abroad, or its internal oppression. Moreover, if pushing back against the mullahs includes imposing new sanctions of any strength, then Washington will potentially face a Tehran walking away from the nuclear deal, creating a crisis that Washington might not be prepared for and doing so in opposition to Europeans who are eager to increase trade with Iran and want the agreement to stand.[21]

Cracking a Would-Be Empire

Locked into an arms-control agreement that was sold in part as a vehicle for moderating Iranian behavior, Washington remains unprepared, if not unwilling, to confront the Middle Eastern power that is trying to transform the region. Many Republicans and Democrats, chastened by the Afghan and Iraq wars, remain allergic to the Middle East. Few in foreign policy circles believe Obama's nuclear deal was a brilliant piece of diplomacy. They just view it the way the president probably did: a means to avoid answering hard questions about war and peace.

Still hooked on the optimistic possibilities of Rouhani, a big slice of the foreign policy establishment in Washington does not want to see the Islamic Republic as an imperial enterprise, and among those who do, some may even find it a positive development. The reasoning: Chaos is awful, and Sunnis have lost their minds (for example, look at the Islamic State, al Qaeda, and a myriad of other primitive radical groups), but Iran comparatively is an island of gradually modernizing stability. The mullahs have not bombed Americans and Europeans outside of a war zone in years and largely restricted their hostages to overly adventurous American backpackers, poorly led US sailors, a hapless retired FBI officer, and dual nationals who have had the bad judgment to visit or work in the Islamic Republic. Since America is not going to intervene militarily to pacify the Middle East, then it is better to have Iran and its Shi'ite allies dominate than Sunni Arabs, who are too divided, weak, politically unstable, or religiously unhinged.[22]

As for the president, Donald Trump has so far given little indication that he sees the Islamic Republic as President Obama did—moderates versus hard-liners. But beyond describing the nuclear deal as dumb and poorly negotiated, Trump has not extensively critiqued the Islamic Republic or its foreign policies. He may view it as a Shi'ite Islamist threat that must be countered militarily, regardless of what happens to the nuclear deal—or not. He may view it as a menace to Persian Gulf oil—or not. Or he may see Iran as a state that nevertheless can be traded with.[23] It is all uncertain.

What is clear, however, is the Islamic Republic and the United States remain fundamentally at odds as regimes; their guiding principles do not amicably coexist. And Iran's success in Iraq, Syria, and Yemen have only whetted the clerical regime's appetite to push forward. In their success, in their hunger to hurt the United States, Israel, and Saudi Arabia, the mullahs may yet provoke Americans, even those who would rather forget about the Middle East.

Moreover, if President Trump is serious about eliminating the Islamic State and its successors and denying al Qaeda further allies, he will have to, directly or indirectly, take up arms against the clerical regime and its Shi'ite proxies. Islamic State 2.0 and al Qaeda 3.0 are a foregone conclusion unless the Shi'ites are checked *or* Iran and its allies obliterate their Sunni foes. And the Islamic Republic simply does not have the Shi'ite resources to definitively beat the Syrian Sunnis; even permanently downing the Sunnis of Iraq will be a demanding task.

But Tehran certainly has the capacity to continue to destabilize the region and sow the sectarian strife that has made the clerical regime for the first time since the revolution a power to be reckoned with far beyond its borders. Sectarian warfare has driven non-Iranian Shi'ites into Tehran's welcoming arms, making the Islamic Republic the dominant power in the Arab Near

East. The founding fathers' revolutionary dreams—a Middle East reordered, anti-American, and following the lead of the Islamic Republic—have never been closer.

The Islamic Republic's ambitions are not complicated. As with the former Soviet Union, defense is offense. Gen. Hamedani's *tour d'horizon* of threats all lead Tehran to intervene throughout the region. And as the regime's internal legitimacy has collapsed, its external drive—the ruling elite's determination to prove its mettle and exert its writ—has increased.

Fearful of a head-on collision with Tehran, Washington can approach the Iranian threat sequentially, as the military strategists Frederick and Kimberly Kagan have advised in their war-gaming against the Islamic State and al Qaeda.[24] The United States first builds up a Sunni Arab force in Syria within an American-protected safe haven near the Jordanian border—far enough away from Iranian-directed forces and the Russians to avoid a direct confrontation. As the US-supported resistance force becomes larger and more effective, superior on the battlefield to the Islamic State and al Qaeda–affiliated groups, it will rally nonradical Sunnis. Eventually judgment day will arrive, however: American soldiers and their Arab allies will face off against Russia, Iran, and Tehran's foreign and Syrian militias. And if that day arrives, significant nonnuclear sanctions will surely follow. The JCPOA, if it is still alive, will expire soon after.

If the United States is unwilling to commit to an anti-Iran ground game in Iraq and Syria—and the Trump administration so far appears determined to avoid such commitments—then there will be no real pushback against Tehran. What Obama declined to do and gave up in Syria and Iraq will not be coming back. Buoyed by its victories in Syria and Iraq, Tehran will surely try to spark greater violence against the ruling families in Saudi Arabia and Bahrain. The thousands of Iraqi, Afghan, and Pakistani Shi'ites whom the Iranians have deployed will likely become permanent auxiliaries of the Revolutionary Guards.

The Iranian intelligence ministry and the Guards are certainly already sifting through volunteers for clandestine operatives. When they go home, they will recruit and train others, expanding the Iranian network throughout the Greater Middle East. The Islamic State and al Qaeda have built up affiliates throughout the Muslim world; Iran is probably doing so in a more organized manner.

Washington really has not caught on to how the Iranians are trying to change the game. Compared to the Islamic Republic, Sunni non-state actors can be a lethal nuisance. They drive American and especially European counterterrorist officers nuts. At worst, they draw funds—table scraps—from pillaging the wreckage of failed states and the generosity of rich, anti-Western Gulf Arabs. Iran's Shi'ite imperialists, however, feed off the most talented people in the Muslim Middle East, the only country in the region that has really fused its national identity with religion and its national glory with a higher cause.

If Washington were bright, it would go after the clerical regime where it is the weakest—the fissures in the current amalgam that makes the Islamic Republic. Khamenei lives in fear of the American bully pulpit and its insidious soft power. He literally cannot stop talking about this menace. We should give him far more to talk about. An anti-imperialist American foreign policy ought to target Rouhani's circle, far and away still the most competent and clever theocrats. The Iranian president wants to rescue the regime, not reform it, to expand the tent and the wealth of those who support the system that he has doggedly and ruthlessly supported since the revolution. An ardent supporter of the war in Syria, he wants to advance Tehran's reach throughout the Middle East, using European investment and increasing energy sales to pay for the effort.

In turn, Washington should want to undermine the more vibrant economy that Rouhani has promised. Failed aspirations have always been an excellent kick-starter for domestic upheaval, as we saw again in the recent nationwide, provincial protests. And Iran is a volcano of contradictions. To the extent that it can, Washington should accentuate those contradictions, especially the century-old Iranian quest for representative government.[25]

The Islamic Republic has an irremediable birth defect: Popular sovereignty and theocracy, in theory, coexist. In practice, the clerics try to "manage" democracy. In 2009, as Khamenei has himself admitted, that management proved "a great challenge."[26] Gen. Mohammad Ali Jaafari, commander of the Revolutionary Guard, was even more explicit about the democratic threat. He revealed in a (leaked) videotaped meeting of senior guard officers that the presidential election had to be curtailed given how many reformists had already penetrated the government. "This slope was worrisome, and everyone analyzed that if the trend continued, the election would go to a second round; and in the second round, the outcome would be unpredictable."[27] In a public speech, Jaafari declared that during the Green Movement protests, "the Islamic system went nearly to the border of overthrow."[28] An intelligent American foreign policy would give due attention to the confessions of our enemies. It would start with planning the incremental steps behind any regime-change strategy.

Almost everyone on the left and right actually wants to see the regime change in Iran—to see real popular sovereignty develop. Where people differ, of course, is whether the United States should try to advance the cause and what means it should deploy to help effect the downfall of theocracy. Given the certainty that the Islamic Republic will have an industrial-size uranium-enrichment capacity when the nuclear deal's sunset clauses kick in in under 15 years and given that Rouhani has proudly proclaimed that one of his notable nuclear achievements is the continuing development of the IR-8 advanced centrifuge (once the IR-8 is deployed, with its small, easily concealable cascades, UN monitoring and safeguards will become all but impossible), it behooves Washington to at least plan for the possibility that a malign Islamic Republic could have missile-ready nuclear weapons within 15 years.

Accordingly, we should want to see a popular counterrevolution, à la the Green Movement, succeed. Misagh Parsa of Dartmouth makes a convincing case that the Islamic Republic simply cannot reform itself through the type of peaceful evolution that President Obama hopefully envisioned.[29] The Green Movement radicalized within one week: It went from protests seeking transparency and fairness in a disputed presidential election to an explicit revolt against the regime. Those convulsive factors are all still there, as is the regime's intent to brutalize those who aim to change the system.

At a minimum, Washington should plan for this eventuality, for another big eruption of discontent. In covert action, it always takes two to tango. Iranians will not do anything they do not want to do; Americans can only suggest things that Iranians themselves believe are worthwhile and practicable. If the theocracy goes down, it will be because millions of Iranians will it. It is long past time for Washington to treat the Islamic Republic as it treated the Soviet Union: We should have a strategy to contain and collapse our enemy. And as with the USSR, we should not allow arms-control agreements to blind us to the ultimate objective.

In Washington's continuing tug-of-war with the mullahs, the Iranian people have remained an untapped resource. When the Green Movement first took to the streets, Iranian youths, who had misinterpreted Obama's Cairo speech, called out to the young president. Playing with his name in Persian, they hoped he was *u ba ma*—"he is with us." He was not.

It is hard to imagine Donald Trump taking the bully pulpit or using sanctions on behalf of these people. Supporting democracy among Muslims is not his thing. But events make a presidency. As the Islamic Republic's Shi'ite imperialism continues to advance, an American containment strategy may well develop. Cracking Shi'ite fraternity in Arab lands will not be easy since Shi'ite-hating Sunnis are all around. Inside Iran, however, this fraternity is far from rock-solid. The appeal of democracy is stronger.

Notes

1. Fars News Agency, "Brother Describes Iran's Quds Force Commander Gen. Soleimani as Kind, Emotional Man," August 26, 2015, http://en.farsnews.com/newstext.aspx?nn=13940603001670.

2. National Commission on Terrorist Attacks Upon the United States, *The 9/11 Commission Report* (New York: W. W. Norton, 2004), 61–62. This contact evolved into training missions in the Islamic Republic and the Bekaa Valley in Lebanon in the early 1990s. Contact continued after Osama bin Ladin relocated from Khartoum to Afghanistan in 1996. Evidence strongly suggests that no fewer than eight of the 14 Saudis who participated in the 9/11 operation had traveled through Iran in the year before the attack. National Commission on Terrorist Attacks Upon the United States, *The 9/11 Commission Report*, 240–42.

3. Utaq Khabar, "Akherin musahabeh-ye sardar hamedani dar mowred-e suriye va fitneh 88," July 18, 1394, otaghkhabar24.ir/print/18722. Translated by the author.

4. Utaq Khabar, "Akherin musahabeh-ye sardar hamedani dar mowred-e suriye va fitneh 88."

5. *Sa'at-e 16 be vaqt-e halab, ravayetha'i az zandegi-ye ustad-e jengha-ye namutaqaren-e mehvar-e muqavamat*, Tehran, Nashr-e 27, 1394. Translated by the author.

6. For an excellent discussion of what was, see Mehran Kamrava, *Iran's Intellectual Revolution* (Cambridge, UK: Cambridge University Press, 2008).

7. See, for example, Farhad Khosrokhavar and Olivier Roy, *Iran: Comment sortir d'une révolution religieuse* [Iran: How to escape a religious revolution] (Paris: Éditions du Seuil, 1999). This is the best book on the challenges of peaceful political evolution in the Islamic Republic written during that period.

8. Misagh Parsa, *Democracy in Iran: Why It Failed and How It Might Succeed* (Cambridge, MA: Harvard University Press, 2016), 17.

9. For the best descriptions of the Green Movement and its enormous impact, see Parsa, *Democracy in Iran*. It is worthwhile for the reader to compare the dimensions of the Green Revolt with the Islamic Revolution. To do so, juxtapose Parsa's commentary with the excellent analysis of the Islamic Revolution in Charles Kurzman, *The Unthinkable Revolution in Iran* (Cambridge, MA: Harvard University Press, 2005).

10. Parsa, *Democracy in Iran*, 179–205. Parsa's commentary on the doggedness of student dissent is detailed and trenchant.

11. Parsa, *Democracy in Iran*, 17.

12. Constance Arminjon Hachem, *Chiisme et État: Les clercs à l'épreuve de la modernité* (Paris: CNRS Éditions, 2013), 500. Translated from French by the author.

13. See Center for Human Rights in Iran, "Iranian Student: Are We on the Right Side in Syria?," Facebook, translated by Amir Toumaj, December 8, 2016, https://www.facebook.com/iranhumanrights.org/videos/10154009774815841/.

14. Akbar Ganji, "Syria: The War on Development and Democracy," Huffington Post, January 7, 2014, http://www.huffingtonpost.com/akbar-ganji/syria-the-war-on-developm_b_4556744.html.

15. Ali Alfoneh (nonresident senior fellow, Atlantic Council), email message to author, April 17, 2017. Alfoneh derives his figures from tracking funeral announcements for

fallen members of the corps. According to Alfoneh, the command structure between the Quds Force and mainline units has become interchangeable if not indistinguishable.

16. For an intriguing discussion on political legitimacy and salvation in early Islam, see Patricia Crone, *God's Rule: Government and Islam: Six Centuries of Medieval Islamic Political Thought* (New York: Columbia University Press, 2004), 17–33.

17. See CNN Library, "Syrian Civil War Fast Fact," updated April 9, 2017, http://www.cnn.com/2013/08/27/world/meast/syria-civil-war-fast-facts/index.html; and United Nations High Commissioner for Refugees, "Syrian Regional Refugee Response," accessed May 4, 2017, http://data.unhcr.org/syrianrefugees/regional.php.

18. See United Nations Security Council, "Resolution 2231 (2015): Arms-Related Transfers," www.un.org/en/sc/2231/restrictions-arms.shtml.

19. President Obama's Middle Eastern National Security Council staff, in discussion with the author, Summer 2014.

20. Saeed Ghasseminejad, "Iran's Revolutionary Guard Gets a Raise," Foundation for Defense of Democracies, April 3, 2017, http://www.defenddemocracy.org/media-hit/saeed-ghasseminejad-irans-revolutionary-guard-gets-a-raise/.

21. Concerning Iranian threats to walk away from the deal, see IRNA, "Zarif: Jomhuri-ye Islami-ye Iran az amadegi-ye kamel baraye bazgasht be sharayet qabl az BARJAM barkhordar ast," 30 Esfand 1395, http://www.irna.ir/esfahan/fa/News/82470128/.

22. To get a sense of this "pro-Iran" sentiment, read essays about Iran and Syria in both the *New York Review of Books* and the *American Conservative*. Although the journalist Christopher de Bellaigue, the *Review's* most elegant writer on the Islamic Republic, and Patrick Buchanan, a founding editor of the *American Conservative*, are universes apart, they both are essentially pro-Iran in their discussion of the Middle East, including the war in Syria. In sync with the populist right, the *American Conservative* has perhaps the most constant voice for recasting Iran as a nonthreatening enemy or even a potential ally. Fox's Tucker Carlson appears to be moving in the same direction. On the left, the liberal writer Peter Beinart regularly depicts Iran as an anti–Islamic State/anti-Sunni jihadist force for good in the Middle East. The *New Yorker* journalist Robin Wright, who is a fan of Iranian Foreign Minister Mohammad-Javad Zarif, consistently writes favorably about Iran under Rouhani. Or see the commentary of former senior US officials Jessica Mathews and Thomas Pickering, who both regularly write on Iran in the *New York Review of Books* and who never dwell on the clerical regime's actions in Syria and Iraq, preferring to keep the spotlight firmly on the soundness of the nuclear agreement. This preference has become almost de rigueur among the liberal foreign policy set. A pro-Iran, pro-engagement (but anti-hard-line mullah) sentiment is also notable at the *New York Times*, which sponsors for-profit tourism to the Islamic Republic. It is difficult to imagine the *New York Times* doing such trips today to Putin's Russia. The richness of Persian culture has something to do with this moral blind spot. (The advertising I have seen for these trips does not mention Iran's brutal suppression of dissidents; the persecution of the Baha'i, Jews, and homosexuals; or the vast slaughter that the clerical regime has abetted in Syria.) See Reuel Marc Gerecht, "Radioactive Regime: Iran and Its Apologists," *Weekly Standard*, May 20, 2013, http://www.weeklystandard.com/radioactive-regime/article/722050.

23. To date, the Trump administration has been notably quiet about Boeing's $17 billion sale of aircraft to Iran.

24. Jennifer Cafarella, Frederick W. Kagan, and Kimberly Kagan, "America's Way Ahead in Syria," AEI's Critical Threats Project and Institute for the Study of War, March 14, 2017, https://www.aei.org/publication/americas-way-ahead-in-syria/.

25. With this in mind, Parsa's *Democracy in Iran* may be the single most important book in English since the Islamic Revolution.

26. See Parsa, *Democracy in Iran*, 249.

27. Parsa, *Democracy in Iran*, 249.

28. Parsa, *Democracy in Iran*, 250.

29. See Parsa's discussion of reform versus revolution. Parsa, *Democracy in Iran*, 290–321.

4

Not a Trap but a Minefield:
The Thucydidean Challenge
to American Foreign Policy

WALTER RUSSELL MEAD

Try as we may to get past him, Thucydides keeps writing himself back into the historical narrative. Twenty-five years ago, the American foreign policy establishment was celebrating the "end of history" and hailing a new era of peace and development. Economics would no longer be a "dismal science," as the benefits of free trade brought prosperity to all, and geopolitics would fade away, as policymakers around the world focused on constructing a lasting liberal order and a democratic peace.

At the dawn of the Trump era, the world no longer looks so benign. The Middle East has exploded into some of the worst violence since World War II, China has clearly embarked on a revisionist course in Asia, and Russia seeks to dismantle the post–Cold War order in Europe. American policymakers struggle to get to grips with an eruption of challenges around the world, even as they are flabbergasted by the election results at home. The liberal world order no longer seems as global, as orderly, or as liberal as we expected it to be. We have never needed Thucydides more nor wanted him less.

Thucydides, as always, is our best guide to disappointment. When euphoria fades, we return to the ironic, complex prose of the Father of History and ask ourselves how the grim Athenian would view our current state. Indeed, as tensions have risen in Asia, no less an authority than Xi Jinping has invoked Thucydides by name to describe the current state of US-China relations, asking whether the United States and China are caught in a "Thucydides Trap."[1] Like many who cite him, Xi raises the specter of Thucydides only to dismiss him: "There is no such thing as the so-called Thucydides trap in the world. But should major countries time and again make the mistakes of strategic miscalculation, they might create such traps for themselves."[2]

Xi is partly right. The Thucydides Trap, as it appears in the US-China policy debate, is a radically stripped down and oversimplified abstraction loosely inspired by Thucydides' work. It does not really correspond to what happened between Athens and Sparta, and it is even less adequate when used as a framework to describe US-Chinese relations or world politics today.

Thucydides, however, whose name is often taken in vain by those who hope to invoke his prestige without coming to grips with his thought, remains an essential thinker for understanding world politics, especially now. He may not have the last word on the problems around us, but the insights he offers help clarify our dilemmas and illuminate our options. Yet to grapple with Thucydides requires us to step outside the ideological comfort zone of the American mind.

There are three dominant strains in American foreign policy thought: liberalism, realism, and, underlying and connecting them both, rationalism, a belief that rational actors making rational choices shape history. Thucydides rejects all three viewpoints. His history offers what in many ways remains the most serious critique of liberal optimism about democracy, commerce, and trade.

But it is not only liberal pieties that Thucydides undermines; the realism of the Father of History is a more complex and in some ways darker vision than the set of ideas and assumptions labeled realist in the contemporary academic world. Beyond that, the bleak Thucydidean view about the limited powers of human reason to chart a safe course through the storms of history challenges some of the deepest assumptions at the heart of American statecraft.

In the quarter century since the end of the Cold War, American policy under both Republican and Democratic presidents has been largely informed by liberal assumptions. We sought to create a lasting world order on the foundations of free government, free trade, and the free flows of information and capital.

For liberalism, democracy and commerce are the foundation stones on which the future happiness of humanity will rest. Democracy is the best form of government, leading to policies that, whatever short-term wobbles there may be, protect the material and security interests of citizens better over the long haul than any alternative form of government. Capitalism, modified by political pressure so that the poor are not utterly left behind, creates wealth, and since the mass of the people seek wealth, they will use their democratic power to elect governments that support capitalism.

Economically successful democratic states are also more peaceful than other regime types. Democracy leads, on the whole, to better policies, and better policies lead to greater prosperity and more peace. Promoting democracy and a liberal economic order abroad is, therefore, at the center of the national interest.

Liberalism in the modern sense did not exist in Thucydides' time, but that does not prevent his history from challenging its core beliefs. Athens was a democracy, and in Thucydides' telling it was the bad decisions the democracy made that caused the city to lose a war it ought to have won. The democracy chose weak leaders and bad men; it was dazzled by Alcibiades but easily dissuaded from following him at the first real crisis.

Moreover, its internal democratic politics did not prevent Athens from the most ruthless policies abroad. It was the aristocratic party that favored moderation when punishing the rebels of Myteline, while the democracy voted for genocide. Later, when the democracy was stronger, it was democratically elected officials who presided over the mass murder of the Melians. Far from being peace loving, the democrats were consistently more aggressive than the aristocrats, and the democratic voters supported the policies that broke the Peace of Nicias.

From the Thucydidean perspective, democracy is not only no more peaceful than any other form of government but also unstable. Democracy does not last. Sooner or later, the foolish mob will fling itself into the arms of a plausible liar who promises everything, as he enriches himself and entrenches himself in power.

In the age of Putin, Erdoğan, Orbán, Chávez, and, some would argue, Trump, this argument may seem stronger than it did in 1990. We are beginning to remember that democracy often leads to populism and chauvinism and that the economic and security policies democracies vote for often do not work. That can lead to a vicious cycle: Bad policies voted in by democratic majorities increase social strain. That strain makes democratic politics more radical and less rational, leading to the election of worse leaders with worse policies.

As for the related liberal idea that commerce smooths international relations by creating common interests in win-win outcomes, again Thucydides offers a skeptical counter-vision. It is the commercial, trading cities that triggered the Peloponnesian War. Sparta was a status-quo power. It had no real desire to extend its power and was content to mind its own business. Corcyra, a city in northwest Greece that controlled much of the trade to Italy and beyond, thanks to its geographical position, came into conflict with Corinth, which was historically the most important trading and maritime state on the west coast of Greece. When the Athenians intervened, eager to add Corcyra's naval power to their own and constrain Corinthian power, the Corinthians approached Sparta to demand assistance. Trade was a destabilizing factor in Thucydidean Greece; it threatened the balance of power, intensified old conflicts, created new ones, and provided rival states with the resources for wars of greater scope and more destructiveness than ever before.

That 25 years of liberal order building has created a disorderly and conflict-prone world would come as no surprise to Thucydides. Democracy, he would argue, makes states more irritable, less rational, and less predictable. Commerce increases the likelihood of rivalries and conflict even as it gives states the means to prepare for war.

Contemporary realists are well aware of the Thucydidean critiques of liberal thought. Indeed, Thucydides is one of the authorities to whom realists returned in the early Cold War to counter the intellectual hegemony of liberalism in American strategic thought.

But Thucydides was no realist in the modern, American, and academic sense of that term. Modern realists have shifted from Thucydides' direct criticism of democracy as being less well suited than other forms of government to preserving peace and stability to a studied indifference to regime type. This might be unavoidable in the American context; it would be difficult to reach high office in the United States while openly scoffing at democratic dogma. But the "realism" that results is a weak and denatured creature, compared to the complex vision of Thucydidean realism, and the costs to analytic coherence are serious.

No concept could be less congenial to Thucydides than the idea that domestic politics and regime type are largely irrelevant to the study of international relations. The central focus of Thucydides' analysis of the Athenian defeat in the Peloponnesian War is the relationship between Athenian foreign and domestic policy. Thucydides believes that domestic politics matter enormously in foreign policy and that regime type can often affect states' foreign policy choices. He would dismiss with contempt the idea that internal politics were irrelevant to foreign policy or that the structure of the international system determined states' policies.

Even if we take the classic Thucydidean idea behind Xi Jinping's question—rising power and the fear that it caused in Sparta—we see that for Thucydides the security dilemma is shaped by the way the domestic political structure of the two states affects the international system. Sparta was a status-quo power because the way it was structured domestically gave it no choice. The Spartiate elite that gave Sparta its military edge was limited in size due to the great length of time and amount of training necessary to produce new members. Its military strategy had to be cautious, as without a large reserve at home, there was no protection against a helot rebellion. Sparta was a conservative structure, built to last but not to grow.

This domestic set of arrangements, not the structure of international politics, determined Sparta's basic attitude toward rising Athenian power. Sparta could not compete with Athens in a world of rising powers; it could only try to prevent Athens from creating a new kind of power in Greece. By its nature, Sparta could not grow to compete in a world of mega-city-states. Athens aspired to transcend the scale of Greek city-state politics to construct a larger empire—perhaps with the example of Carthage in mind. Because of the limits that its domestic institutions imposed on its foreign policy, Sparta could not compete with Athens by attempting to construct a counterweight; it could only hope to maintain its independence by blocking the Athenian drive for greatness.

Given its own domestic politics, Athens on the other hand could not accept the limitation on its ambitions that was necessary to defuse Spartan hostility. Athens supported a large and growing population on the poor soils of Attica. Much of its population depended on trade and the fruits of empire for its prosperity. (Before the war, Pericles used the proceeds of the allied contributions to the Delian League for a vast public works building program in Athens, providing employment and income to his constituents.)

The large urban population had achieved substantial political power and naturally pushed Athenian foreign policy in directions that met the needs of the tradesmen and townsmen who controlled a majority in the assembly. The Athenian majority needed an expansive commercial policy to prosper, and its definition of its security requirements included a concern for the trade routes to the Black Sea granaries that provide the cheap grain that the population could not live without. Given the presence of Persia, Macedonia, and various barbarian kingdoms along those vulnerable trade routes, Athens had to aspire to a level of military power that inevitably threatened Sparta's claims in Greece.

The Thucydides Trap is not a product of the structure of the international system of the day; it is a product of the interplay between the structure of the international system and the domestic political structures of the states involved. The war that followed was similarly shaped by the domestic political systems of the two states and their allies.

In Athens, Pericles' strategy of naval mobilization and masterly inactivity in land warfare weakened the aristocratic landholding families—their property was destroyed and incomes affected when Spartan forces, unopposed, burned their homes and farms in the surrounding countryside—and strengthened the democratic, urban elements, who benefited from ship building and supply orders and the daily pay given to oarsmen. The different economic impacts of the war on different Athenian constituencies played a significant role in the later development of Athenian strategy.

On the one hand, the aristocrats (such as Nicias) became a peace party, looking for a compromise with Sparta to end a war whose destructive power they fully felt. On the other, democratic politicians such as Cleon favored intensifying the war effort and found it easy to win support among the urban voters, whose livelihood depended on a steady stream of government orders and military pay. In the later years of the war, democrats continued to favor a policy of war and resistance. The aristocrats preferred peace, even a peace that limited Athenian ambitions abroad. For them, defeat by Sparta meant victory over democratic opponents at home.

Spartan strategy was governed equally profoundly by the nature of Spartan society. Preserving the Spartan ruling stratum—the leading families and the Spartiates who, having successfully undergone the rigorous training required of freeborn, purebred Spartan boys, were the political and military basis of the state—was the primary object of Spartan war policy. After the defeat at Pylos, when more than 100 Spartiates were captured by Athenian forces, the need to free these prisoners overrode virtually everything else in Spartan policy, and the country was ready to make an unfavorable peace with Athens to get them back. This was not mere sentimentality; the Spartan elite was so small and its numbers grew so slowly that the loss of the force at Pylos significantly weakened the city's ability to fight.

Meanwhile, domestic politics shaped other cities' decisions to align with either Athens or Sparta. The democratic and oligarchic factions in city-states across Greece saw a reflection of their domestic rivalries in the international rivalry between mercantile, democratic Athens and conservative, agrarian Sparta. The dueling political ideologies of the day were rooted in the economic and social structures of the city-states. The aristocratic faction by and large consisted of the old, large, landholding families in each city. The democratic faction represented a mix of traders and urban dwellers whose livelihoods depended on the extension of foreign trade. The Spartan vision of a Greece of stable, traditional city-states matched aristocratic preferences; the Athenian vision was tailor-made for democracies.

The Thucydidean state is no billiard ball, bouncing across the table in response to external forces. The state is more like an organism whose internal metabolism provides a set of needs that it seeks to satisfy through action in its environment. Those actions can change the environment; there is a constant and ever-shifting interplay between states' domestic politics and the nature of their relations with one another.

There are, then, points of agreement and disagreement between Thucydides and our contemporary liberals and realists. Like liberals, Thucydides believes that regime type matters; like them he believes that there are differences between democratic and nondemocratic states and differences between commercial and noncommercial powers. Unlike liberals, however, he does not think that democracy and commerce per se provide a stronger foundation for international peace.

Like realists, he believes that calculations of interest normally trump ethical imperatives and that this is as true for democratic and commercial states as for any other kind. But he disagrees with realists that regime type is irrelevant; different regime types define their interests differently and make different choices among strategic options based on the needs of their domestic political structure. Beyond this, he would argue that for many regimes the chief object of policy is preserving regime power at home rather than some kind of national interest abroad. Both the democrats and oligarchs of the Peloponnesian War period were ready to sacrifice the interests of their city to secure the survival or prosperity of their faction.

But there is a deeper difference between the Thucydidean approach to politics and that of both liberal and realist contemporary scholars. Modern analysts tend to be much more confident in the role of reason in human affairs than Thucydides was, and they give a much lower place to the effects of the unknown and uncontrollable factors such as fortune or fate, which profoundly shaped the limits within which Thucydides believed that human will and strategy must work.

The world of modern political theory is a much cleaner and simpler place than the one Thucydides believed he inhabited. Both liberal internationalists and modern realists believe, for example, that states can determine their true interests with clarity and certainty and that they will then for the most part discern and choose policies that advance and defend those interests. Thucydides did not believe human beings could be counted on to behave like rational actors; they frequently do not know what is in their best interests, and they do not always choose the policies that would advance their interests, rationally considered.

Thucydidean history is not a realm in which rational actors calmly analyze their choices and then make considered decisions among them. In the world of Thucydides, people are moved by superstition, fear, jealousy, and a thousand other emotions. But they are not only the victims of their own passions; they are also the playthings of fortune. In the world of Thucydides, chance plays such a major role that the actions of human beings are only one factor, and by no means always the most important factor, in determining the fate of states.

To take the most obvious example, had there not been an outbreak of plague in Athens, the war would likely have taken a very different course. Not only would Athens' resources have been significantly greater, but the guiding hand of Pericles would also have kept Athenian policy on a more sensible course. Similarly, had Athens not succumbed to panic on the eve of the Sicilian Expedition, Alcibiades would likely have remained in command, and his more forceful leadership might well have succeeded where the hesitancy and timidity of Nicias failed. Shifts in the wind determined the outcome of important naval battles, and a lunar eclipse delayed Nicias' retreat from Syracuse and made the ensuing disaster more likely.

What this means in practical terms is that a Thucydidean would always bear in mind the limited use of political theory in forecasting or shaping events. History, for the Thucydidean, is not a contest in which the rewards usually go to the participant who deduces a set of propositions about how the world works and then shapes his conduct by referring to them. Fortune can intervene at any moment and upset the calculations of the most theoretically sound. "Inevitable" is not a word to be used when it comes to the relationship of human actions and historical events. Between the act and the result lies the realm of chance, in which forces no human understands or can control act to determine the result.

The strict limits in which human beings are free to determine their own fate has long preoccupied historical writers. From the time of Sun Tzu to that of Clausewitz, those who have tried to analyze foreign policy and conflict devoted much of their energy to the question of fate and chance: the limits that events outside of human control place on human agency. Cesare Borgia, writes Machiavelli, did everything right and would have established a permanent principality for the Borgia family, had he not fallen gravely ill at the time of his father's unexpected and premature demise.[3] Clausewitz makes friction one of the key elements in his analysis of war and never lets his readers forget the vast gap between the theory and practice of war.[4]

Both liberals and realists in contemporary America, in contrast, see history as a more transparent medium and believe in a clearer connection between what people attempt and what they achieve. If you choose appropriate goals and follow the correct procedures, more often than not your results should match your intentions.

For Thucydides, the link between cause and effect is murkier. Given the role of fortune in human affairs, being "right" is not as important as being lucky. In Thucydides' estimation, Nicias was a good man, but after a long run of good fortune, he was overtaken by ill fortune outside the walls of Syracuse. Cleon was a bad man and a bad general, but fortune smiled on him at crucial moments. Pericles was a brilliant leader with a brilliant war strategy for Athens, but fate struck Athens with a plague that took Pericles—and left Thucydides to tell the story of the new and unexpected world of Athenian struggle after the plague had passed.

For Thucydides, it is never enough to be right. Politics is unpredictable and largely governed by chance. Alcibiades was a meteor streaking across the sky; both his successes and his failures lay beyond the scope of normal theory. He was able at different periods to impose his personal agenda on the state, an agenda that often bore little resemblance to the national interest conventionally understood.

The twin beliefs that most actors are rational and that the role of chance in human interactions is limited lie at the basis of the technocratic state. It is not surprising that in our times most thinkers on international affairs make robust assumptions about the relationship of theory and praxis—that orthodoxy leads to orthopraxis, which leads to the end state that theory predicts. If the Federal Reserve has the right monetary theory and takes the actions that theory prescribes, the economy will behave as the textbooks tell us it will. If we understand the nature of the international system and apply those principles consistently to the policy process, our foreign policies will achieve the results that we seek.

These beliefs, common today in policy circles but rare among sophisticated observers before the Enlightenment, are so deeply engrained in our habits of thought that it is difficult for many moderns to imagine how the world looks without the comfort and assurance they bring. To some degree, the rise of these beliefs attests to real changes in the human condition. If Clausewitz were to catch cholera in eastern Germany today, he would be successfully treated and go on to finish *On War*. As infant mortality rates decline, as fewer women die in childbirth, as more infectious diseases yield ground to advancing medicine, we no longer feel quite as vulnerable to fortune and chance.

Yet the specters of chance and irrationality have not been banished as effectively as one might hope. The possibility that an accidental nuclear exchange could lead to a conflagration ending civilization haunted both superpowers during the Cold War, and rightly so. After a long post–World War II period of relative stability, the economic crisis of 2008 and 2009 reminded us rather sharply that our technocratic economists cannot insulate us from destabilizing shocks originating in irrational and unpredictable interaction among forces and instruments we do not fully understand. In many ways, events in the post–Cold War world have been drifting away from the more controlled and "rational" patterns of the Cold War.

The deepening world crisis through which we are living today suggests that a new look at Thucydidean skepticism about the modern dogmas of liberalism, realism, and rationalism may be in order. It remains to be seen whether the current difficulties represent a passing moment of instability, as the world struggles to regain its balance, or something more meaningful and dangerous. But in either case, it is useful to see how the Thucydidean critique of the foundations of modern foreign policymaking can illuminate the difficulties American foreign policy faces in the principal theaters of world politics.

In the Middle East, neither liberalism, modern realism, nor rationalism has served American policymakers particularly well; the United States must cope with a set of problems that resist liberal and realist analysis. In Asia, the attempt to construct a liberal order and integrate China into the international system as a responsible stakeholder has come up against some intractable problems. In the Atlantic world, where the process of liberal order building has had the most success and gone the furthest, the difficulties of both the United States and the European Union raise basic questions about the future of American strategy.

The Minefield in the Middle East

In no region of the world has the United States deployed more resources and devoted more time and energy to less positive effect than in the Middle East. After the expensive and inconclusive conflicts of the Bush era and the disappointing results of its democratization efforts in the Palestinian territories and elsewhere, the Obama administration failed to develop a coherent or sustainable policy for the region, attempting to build bridges to Sunni Islam while tilting toward Iran, mistaking Erdoğan for the longed-for "democratic Islamist" leader who would domesticate Islamist politics within a liberal framework, and misreading the Arab Spring as the beginning of an age of democratic transition. The "liberal meliorist" framework so deeply engrained in American thinking fails to engage with the facts on the ground in a constructive manner. The outlook has conspicuously been unable to generate successful lines of policy.

The liberal meliorist looks at problems in the Middle East, such as terrorism and religious radicalism, and applies boilerplate liberal ideology to them. Terrorism and religious radicalism in the Middle East are caused by poverty and oppression. Liberal economic and political policies, shaped by the technocratically gifted in the light of the best peer-reviewed research of the day, are the solution. The objection that the United States has been promoting liberal solutions in the Middle East since World War II with no discernable impact on the problem is dismissed on one of two grounds: either that the United States has not promoted liberal policies consistently enough (support for authoritarian regimes, miserly foreign aid allocations) or that it has used the wrong technocrats with the wrong programs.

The failed maxims of yesteryear (import substitution strategies, military-guided modernization strategies, land reform, capital market liberalization, etc.) must be discarded. The brilliant new strategies hot off the presses and embodying the latest formulations of conventional American academic wisdom will address our current policy problems by working such a benign and fundamental transformation in the Middle East that all will be well.

For the liberal meliorist, today is always a day of opportunity, and the shiny new economic and social development theories (Promotion of inclusive civil society organizations! Gender-based development policies! Training democracy activists!) will correct the defects of the shopworn and bedraggled old theories whose failures lie scattered across the landscape.

The grim Thucydidean reality in the Middle East is that so far as we can know, neither prosperity nor democracy is going to arrive soon enough to make any practical difference to the problems that we confront there. There is essentially nothing American foreign policy can do about this. We cannot bring democracy to Libya, and we cannot make Yemen or Pakistan prosperous. No diplomatic issue has engaged as much American attention and muscle since the 1970s as the effort to end the Arab-Israeli dispute; we are farther from a comprehensive settlement today than we were in 1992. We cannot alter the political trajectory of Turkey, we cannot disentangle the Egyptian state from the country's corrupt and rentier economy, and we cannot introduce the institutions and practices of European and Atlantic history into a different region of the world with either bayonets or bank transfers. There may be good reasons for continuing some of these diplomatic and aid efforts, but it would be extremely foolish to think that the root causes of Middle Eastern terrorism and strife will somehow disappear in a policy-relevant time frame.

Yet realism also has its limits. The weakness of Middle Eastern states means that some of the region's most important problems simply cannot be addressed through the usual realist channels of state-to-state diplomacy.

Many of the Gulf states, for example, are so concerned by the potential internal threat of religious opposition that they purchase peace at home in two ways: They tolerate the educational and religious activities of radical groups at home so long as such activities are not targeted against the current rulers, and they allow their citizens to fund and fight for radical causes beyond the frontier. This approach, deeply damaging to American and other Western interests, is in some cases something these governments could not change even if they so wanted. An uneasy truce with religious radicalism is a condition of their existence, and no foreign pressure can persuade them to follow what the regimes believe would be a suicidal policy of confrontation with forces they cannot control.

Liberals are right to point to transnational problems as the root causes of many of the conditions in the Middle East of most concern to the United States and its allies and associates and to note that cooperation with undemocratic and corrupt states will in some cases make those problems worse. Realists are right that the liberal approaches have failed and are almost certain to continue to fail. The Middle East, in other words, is a Thucydidean space, not a modern one. Neither the liberal quest for cures nor the realist quest for deals offers the United States a safe path across the minefield of Middle East politics.

Given the Middle East's continuing importance to global energy markets and therefore to the world economy, the United States remains committed to this tumultuous region. It is a minefield that we must carefully and painstakingly traverse. As we do so, it is worth remembering that there are worse guides to its pitfalls than Thucydides.

The Asian Game of Thrones

As in the Middle East, American policy in Asia has mixed liberal and realist elements, but the overall direction has been more clearly and unambiguously liberal. The primary goal of American policy has been to encourage China to join the international system. Liberal carrots such as enhanced access to world markets were mixed with realist sticks, including the maintenance of American military superiority in the region. Simultaneously, even as the United States has focused on security issues in relations with North

Korea, the overall thrust of its regional policy has been to promote democratization and economic liberalization.

In the 1990s, the United States worked to open the door to Chinese participation in the global economy on favorable terms. The hope was that Chinese integration into the global system would lead to smoother US-China relations even as China's economic and therefore military and political power increased. Americans made the case that economic development would inevitably pull China toward democratization and that domestic liberalization would result in a more cooperative foreign policy stance.

Additionally, as China acquired a stake in the global system, it would become a supporter of that system. Germany and Japan became more committed to the international liberal order as their success in it transformed their economic and political standing after World War II. China would, Americans hoped, follow their lead. On the basis of these calculations, the economic opening to China and the promotion of a form of globalization in which cheap Chinese labor and state-assisted companies would enjoy tremendous global advantages became American policy in the 1990s.

A quarter of a century later, it is difficult to argue that the hopes of the early 1990s have been fulfilled. China is more revisionist, less democratic, and less of a responsible stakeholder in the international system than the proponents of the opening expected. China's remarkable economic growth has substantially cut poverty at home, but some of the resources unleashed by its new prosperity have gone into developing an increasingly formidable military machine. China has become a commercial nation and a global trading power, but this transformation does not seem to have made it more pacifistic.

As happened with Athens, Corcyra, and Corinth, the growth of China's trade has given it a new set of interests and new resources with which to pursue them. Fear that the United States or Japan would use sea power to cut China off from vital overseas sources of energy and raw materials drives much of China's strategic thinking. These concerns place a premium on China's ability to project power beyond its neighborhood. Many mercantile powers have pursued active, vigorous, and even aggressive foreign policies over the centuries. China seems at least as likely to follow the path marked out by predecessors such as Britain, Portugal, Venice, and Carthage—to say nothing of Athens itself—as to embrace a liberal ideal in which most Chinese leaders emphatically do not believe.

Meanwhile, it is harder to sustain the liberal faith in the triumph of democracy in Asia. In the late 20th century, democracy appeared to be triumphing across East Asia, as South Korea, Taiwan, the Philippines, and Thailand all moved toward more democratic systems. While democracy remains healthy in South Korea and Taiwan, China appears firmly set on an antidemocratic path, as does Vietnam.

Thailand and the Philippines appear to be moving away from democracy, and in Burma the progress of democracy has stalled, as ethnic conflict with the Rohingyas has moved to the fore. Realistically speaking, a stable authoritarian government in Burma has more ability to protect the unpopular Rohingya minority than a democratic movement conscious of the power of both ethnic nationalism and the Buddhist clergy. In Indonesia the forces of extremism and Islamism are eroding what was once a hopeful experiment in democracy in the world's most populous Muslim-majority country.

The American commitment to liberal trade policy has meanwhile collapsed. The failure of the Trans-Pacific Partnership agreement, repudiated by both presidential candidates in 2016, underscored the domestic limits on American trade policy in the region.

To look at East and Southeast Asia today is to look at a failure—not total as in the Middle East, but real—of liberal transformation. Things may change, but for now it appears that despite some encouraging progress and an unprecedented economic boom that has dramatically improved living conditions for hundreds of millions of people, the political outlook for Asia is darkening. Relations between China and its neighbors are deteriorating, and an arms race is developing, as countries from India to Australia to Japan and both Koreas race to improve their military capabilities.

Nationalism has had a more robust post-1945 history in Asia than in Western Europe. Only in Japan did the experiences of the war create the kind of national rejection of militarism that much of Europe has experienced after the conflicts of the 20th century. In countries such as China, both Koreas, Thailand, and Vietnam, a strongly nationalist political culture remains central to politics and is welcomed by authorities as an important force promoting national cohesion. Even in Japan, public concern over North Korea's nuclear program and the threatening appearance of China is promoting a gradual return to a more nationalistic frame of mind.

A region of powerful nation-states that suspect and compete with one another and that are engaged in an accelerating arms race looks more like Europe in 1910 than Europe in 1990. This is not a post-historical landscape.

Asia also demonstrates the wisdom of Thucydidean skepticism about human beings' ability to predict and therefore control the future. The single most important question for the future of Asian politics is the future of the Chinese economy. Will China make a successful transition to a new kind of economy, eschewing both the middle-income trap and the debt trap that lie before it?

Nobody, including the authorities in Beijing, really understands the risks in a financial system like none other in the history of the world. China's historical experience of economic development is unique, and our information about its economic performance is unreliable. Moreover, its regulators and financial market participants have no experience coping with the upheavals and shocks that other capitalist economies have experienced on the road to growth.

In the past, such conditions have led to terrible economic cataclysms that tested the social and political stability of great nations. Yet our ability to predict what happens in China is little better than that of the ancient Athenians to predict the plague; chance and the unknown will have a larger vote in determining the future of Asia than either liberal or realist calculations made in Washington. The future of China's financial system and economic model, a future that we cannot effectively predict, matters much more for the future of American foreign policy in Asia than the abstract argument about whether liberalism or realism best describes the overall trajectory of international politics.

From all this, one can see that the concept of a Thucydides Trap is too one-dimensional and too mechanistic to capture the range of Thucydidean thinking about the United States and China. A Thucydidean analysis of the relationship between the United States and China would look more closely at the relationship of the internal dynamics in each country to their external policies. What, for example, are the domestic forces that would fight to keep both China and the United States heading in a direction that increased the chances of conflict between them?

This is not just a question of "lobbies" and special pleading. How deeply is China's drive to regional hegemony grounded in the political, cultural, and economic systems that keep China united under Communist Party rule?

How committed is the United States to a vision of world order that cannot tolerate the establishment of a Chinese sphere of influence in East Asia? How are the structural economic and social changes experienced by both countries affecting the approach of each country to foreign policy? How wise and farseeing are the leaders at the helms of the two countries? How secure are they in their power, and how free are their hands?

Such an analysis would also step back from a tight focus on the bilateral relationship to the context around the US-China relationship. The Peloponnesian War did not originate in a bilateral quarrel between Athens and Sparta; it began after Corcyra asked Athens to offer it protection from Corinth. Sparta was initially reluctant to enter the war and might not have done so, had not Corinth made the case that, if Sparta failed to come to its aid in this controversy, Sparta's alliance system would unravel even as Athens rose to new heights. Corinth saw that the Athenian alliance with Corcyra made Athens as powerful in the Adriatic as it was in the Aegean and would give it control of Greece's trade with Italy and Sicily as it already controlled Greek trade with Asia Minor and the Black Sea.

In itself the expansion of Athenian naval power into the Adriatic did not threaten Sparta's security. That expansion was, however, a mortal threat to Corinth's status as a major power, and so it became a threat to the health of the Spartan alliance system. Japan and other countries have a role, quite possibly a decisive one, in the future of US-China relations.

The Crisis of the Democratic West

The greatest problem facing American foreign policy today does not come from external enemies or opponents. Russia, China, North Korea, and Iran do not pose as fundamental a challenge to American strategy as does the state of the democratic West, the United States included. The European Union's failure to deal with either its external threats or its internal problems is testing the strength of the transatlantic partnership, even as the election of Donald J. Trump raises the most fundamental questions about the nature of American foreign policy at a critical time. Both the European Union and the United States met the challenges of the Cold War, but in the years since 1990 the two great engines of the Western world have encountered a new set of difficulties.

In both Europe and the United States, the end of the Cold War was taken to mean the end of history. Liberal capitalism had triumphed over its rivals, and the path to a stable world order based on the principles that won the Cold War lay open. Just as West Germany absorbed East Germany after the Cold War, so would the free world absorb the second and third worlds. The globalization of production and finance, the spread of democracy, and the soft power of the triumphant West would transform the world.

Today we see on both sides of the Atlantic the paradoxes of liberal success. The United States and the European Union have both achieved levels of material prosperity and democratic freedom unmatched on any comparable scale in the history of the world. Yet on both sides of the Atlantic, public opinion seems unwilling to bear the burdens necessary to sustain this happy state of affairs. Europeans' reluctance to invest significantly in defense has been evident for decades, and with the election of Donald Trump, Americans sent an unmistakable message that they are weary of the burdens of world leadership and are questioning the foundations of post–World War II American policy.

A Thucydidean would have no difficulty diagnosing what appear to be standard cases of the democratic disease that helped defeat Athens. This is not a new phenomenon; France, Britain, and the United States all refused to take elementary precautions to defend themselves against Hitler when it was easy. Democratic opinion in France and Britain embraced a policy of vengeance against Germany after World War I, only to switch to appeasement at just the point when vigilance was needed. The natural tendency of democratic societies, Thucydides would argue, is to act on the basis of emotion rather than reason, to favor short-term concerns over serious long-term issues, and to listen to flattering leaders who tell comforting lies.

This is, I think, too simple. Human nature may not have changed since the time of Thucydides, but the world is more complicated than it used to be. Although the democratic West has committed its share of follies, it has also emerged victorious from harsh contests.

Nevertheless, if Americans and Europeans today would be wrong to follow Thucydides blindly, it is at least equally dangerous to ignore him. One should never forget that the Peloponnesian War is the story of a great democracy that cracked under the strain of its foreign affairs. The Thucydides Trap that Americans need to worry most about is at home.

Notes

1. The "Thucydides Trap" is a term of art used by international relations scholars and historians to describe a situation in which the rapid rise in power of one state inevitably leads to competition and conflict with an existing great power. Although the concept emerges from Thucydides' account of the war between Sparta and Athens in his *History of the Peloponnesian War*, Thucydides never uses the word "trap" to describe the dynamic between the two city-states.

2. Xi Jinping, "China-US Ties" (speech, Seattle, WA, September 22, 2015), http://www.chinadaily.com.cn/world/2015xivisitus/2015-09/24/content_21964069.htm.

3. Niccolo Machiavelli, *The Prince* (1532), chap. 7.

4. Carl von Clausewitz, *On War* (1832), book 1, chap. 7.

About the Authors

Dan Blumenthal is the director of Asian studies at the American Enterprise Institute, where he focuses on East Asian security issues and Sino-American relations. He has both served in and advised the US government on China issues for more than a decade. From 2001 to 2004, he served as senior director for China, Taiwan, and Mongolia at the Department of Defense. Additionally, he served as a commissioner on the congressionally mandated US-China Economic and Security Review Commission from 2006 to 2012 and held the position of vice chairman in 2007. He has also served on the Academic Advisory Board of the congressional US-China Working Group and as the John A. van Beuren Chair Distinguished Visiting Professor at the US Naval War College. Blumenthal is the coauthor of *An Awkward Embrace: The United States and China in the 21st Century* (AEI Press, 2012).

Reuel Marc Gerecht is a senior fellow with the Foundation for Defense of Democracies. He was previously a resident fellow at the American Enterprise Institute and the director of the Middle East Initiative at the Project for the New American Century. Earlier, he served as a Middle Eastern specialist in the CIA's Directorate of Operations. He is a contributing editor at the *Weekly Standard* and has been a foreign correspondent for the *Atlantic Monthly* and foreign affairs columnist for the *New Republic*. His books include *The Wave: Man, God, and the Ballot Box in the Middle East* (Hoover Institution Press, 2011); *The Islamic Paradox: Sunni Fundamentalists, Shiite Clerics, and the Coming of Arab Democracy* (AEI Press, 2004), and, under the pseudonym of Edward Shirley, *Know Thine Enemy: A Spy's Journey into Revolutionary Iran* (Farrar Straus & Giroux, 1997).

Frederick W. Kagan is the Robert H. Malott Chair and director of the Critical Threats Project at the American Enterprise Institute. In 2009, he served in Kabul, Afghanistan, on Gen. Stanley McChrystal's strategic assessment team.

He returned to Afghanistan in 2010, 2011, and 2012 to conduct research for Generals David Petraeus and John Allen. In July 2011, Chairman of the Joint Chiefs of Staff Admiral Mike Mullen awarded him the Distinguished Public Service Award, the highest honor the chairman can present to civilians who do not work for the Department of Defense. He is author of the series of reports *Choosing Victory: A Plan for Success in Iraq* (2007) and coauthor of the book *Lessons for a Long War: How America Can Win on New Battlefields* (AEI Press, 2010). Kagan is an associate professor of military history at West Point. He has a Ph.D. in Russian and Soviet military history.

Walter Russell Mead is the James Clarke Chace Professor of Foreign Affairs and Humanities at Bard College and the Distinguished Fellow in American Strategy and Statesmanship for the Hudson Institute. He previously served as the Henry A. Kissinger Senior Fellow for US Foreign Policy at the Council on Foreign Relations. The author of *God and Gold: Britain, America, and the Making of the Modern World* (Vintage, 2008) and *Special Providence: American Foreign Policy and How It Changed the World* (Knopf, 2001), Mead is the Global View columnist at the *Wall Street Journal* and the United States book reviewer for *Foreign Affairs*. His next book, *The Arc of a Covenant: The United States, Israel, and the Fate of the Jewish People,* will be published in 2018.

Gary J. Schmitt is resident scholar and codirector of the Marilyn Ware Center for Security Studies at the American Enterprise Institute (AEI). He is also director of AEI's Program on American Citizenship. Schmitt is a former staff director on the Senate Select Committee on Intelligence, executive director of the President's Intelligence Advisory Board, and executive director of the Project for the New American Century. Among his most recent books in national security are *A Hard Look at Hard Power: Assessing the Defense Capabilities of Key Allies and Security Partners* (Strategic Studies Institute, 2015), *Safety, Liberty and Islamist Terrorism: American and European Approaches to Domestic Counterterrorism* (AEI Press, 2010), and *The Rise of China: Essays on the Future Competition* (Encounter Books, 2009). Schmitt has a B.A. in politics from the University of Dallas and a M.A. and Ph.D. in political science from the University of Chicago.